PASTOR TO PASTOR

James E. Hamill

GOSPEL PUBLISHING HOUSE

SPRINGFIELD, MISSOURI

02-0600

Acknowledgments

We would like to thank the following authors and publishers for permission to quote from their works.

Mary LeGrand Bouma, "The Walking Wounded," *Leadership*. Used by permission of author.

Christianity Today, "The Minister and His Wife," by Ralph M. Smucker (© 1969). Used by permission.

Dr. Robert G. Lee, *Bread From Bellevue Oven* published by Sword of the Lord Publishers, Murfreesboro, TN. Used by permission.

McGraw-Hill Book Company, *The Art of Administration* by Ordway Tead (© 1951). Used by permission.

Roy C. Price, "Building Trust Between Pastor and Congregation," *Leadership*. Used by permission of author.

Pat Valeriano, "A Survey of Ministers' Wives," copyright *Leadership*, Fall 1981. A publication of Christianity Today, Inc. Used by permission.

Warren W. Wiersbe, "Principles Are the Bottom Line," *Leadership*. Used by permission of author.

Chapter 9 was originally published in *And He Gave Pastors* (copyrighted by Gospel Publishing House, 1979) and is used by permission, with minor changes.

Library of Congress Catalog Card Number 85-60248
International Standard Book Number 0-88243-600-7
Printed in the United States of America

Contents

Contents

Foreword

In His divine providence, God has given gifts to the Body: pastors, evangelists, administrators, teachers (Ephesians 4:11). James E. Hamill has served in all these capacities. Yet, few men of his generation have exemplified the pastoral ministry to the degree of this beloved brother.

His ministry spanned more than 50 years and five churches. Yet his name is synonymous with one of our great churches, First Assembly in Memphis, Tennessee, where for 37 years he served as pastor. From a small congregation of 99 people the church grew to over 2,800 members under his leadership.

Through his radio and television ministry, he became "pastor" to countless hundreds throughout the Midsouth area. His administrative skills were honed through six building programs of the congregation. The budget of the church grew from $13,000 at the beginning of his pastorate to some $2 million when he retired in 1981—having become annually subscribed in advance by the congregation early in the history of his pastorate.

His love for people, his example of unswerving faithfulness to the Lord, and his unquestioned integrity have been shining examples for us all. His wisdom and leadership skills have served our Fellowship in many areas of ministry. He has served as a General Presbyter almost continuously since 1938, and for 10 years (1971-81) he was a member of the Executive Presbytery. His practical guidance has been of inestimable value to these bodies throughout the years. In addition, he has served on numerous committees of the Movement.

The thrust of his ministry is to proclaim the gospel of Jesus Christ to every creature. As a pastor, his heart beat with evangelism, and his ministry in more than 60 countries of the world always kept this basic.

It is my privilege to commend this book to other pastors and young ministers, for here is a ministry proven in the fire of experience, tested by the years of time, and victorious because of the dedication and commitment of this great pastor—James E. Hamill.

THOS. F. ZIMMERMAN
GENERAL SUPERINTENDENT
ASSEMBLIES OF GOD

Preface

Shortly before I retired from the pastorate of First Assembly of God, Memphis, I received a letter from my longtime friend E. M. Clark, who suggested that it would be helpful to Bible college students and young pastors if I would share with them more than a half century of ministry. I facetiously replied, "Yes, I could tell them about a great number of things that did not work for me."

If those who read this book are like the Athenians in Paul's day, "looking for a new thing," they will doubtless be disappointed. This book is not a list of new ideas, methods, and programs. It is not a magic formula to build a superchurch, nor a panacea for church problems, but an attempt to deal with the fundamental needs of all congregations, large and small.

Pastor to Pastor is a sincere effort to deal with the pastor's magnificent privileges and opportunities as well as his awesome responsibilities and obligations, and to discuss his relationships to God, his family, and his staff, among others, and his involvement with finance, administration, church growth, and the like.

I would like to express my sincere gratitude to all those who encouraged and assisted me in this undertaking, especially Frank Martin, pastor, and Berry Terry, business administrator, of First Assembly of God, Memphis, who provided office equipment and personnel; to Mrs. Billie Faye Hillyard who typed, retyped, and typed again these many pages; and to Emmett Maum and Virginia McDaniel who proofread the manuscript.

1

The Pastor:
His Relationship to God

All ministry—all spiritual work—begins with God. Without a proper relationship to God, a person has no hope of realizing any measure of genuine success in the ministry. He must have a call, a mission, and an experience. He must be obedient, attentive, and committed.

A Call of God

The pastor should be divinely called to preach and teach the gospel. I cannot believe that Jesus made the distinction between laity and clergy that the church later instituted and that we sometimes make today. However, I do believe a difference exists in the qualifications and the responsibilities of those who are called to full-time ministry and those who are not. The New Testament makes this evident.

When the Jerusalem congregation grew to the point of having an administrative problem in its benevolences, the Twelve solved it by calling for an appointment of laymen. This was done in order that the apostles could continue giving "full time to prayers and the work of preaching" (Acts 6:4, TEV).

Paul tells us in Ephesians 4:11 that the Lord has set in the church apostles, teachers, evangelists, and pastors. And in 1 Timothy 3:1-7 he gives the qualifications for a bishop, or "overseer" (NIV), or "presiding elder" (Jerusalem), or "church leader" (TEV). Paul also speaks of the ordination of Timothy by the laying on of hands of the presbytery (1 Timothy 4:14). So the New Testament church did have those who were set apart, ordained, and sent out as full-time ministers of the gospel.

Paul himself, one of the all-time great preachers, knew he was called and ordained of God, as he points out to the Colossians (1:25), "I am made a minister, according to the dispensation of God." The Revised Standard Version reads, "I became a minister according to the divine office which was given to me." Phillips paraphrases this verse, "I am a minister of the Church by divine commission, a commission granted to me for your benefit, and for a special purpose: that I might fully declare God's Word."

Paul establishes his authority as a minister of the gospel in the very first statement to the Colossians when he says, "Paul, an apostle of Jesus Christ by the will of God" (1:1). Of the thirteen Epistles that we know Paul wrote, he begins eleven with such terms as "Paul, a servant of Jesus Christ, called to be an apostle, separated unto the gospel of God" (Romans 1:1). "Paul, called to be an apostle of Jesus Christ through the will of God" (1 Corinthians 1:1). "Paul, an apostle, (not of men, neither by man, but by Jesus Christ, and God the Father, who raised him from the dead)" (Galatians 1:1).

From his prison cell in Rome, the Apostle begins his letter to Philemon with, "Paul, a prisoner of Jesus Christ." Even though Paul had been incarcerated by the Romans and was at that time in a prison cell, he never once talked about being a prisoner of Rome, but "a prisoner of Jesus Christ." He is saying in effect, "I am held by Jesus Christ; I am a love-slave; I am imprisoned by His call to preach the unsearchable riches of Christ; I do not recognize any other bondage; I do not admit that I am held by any other power; I do not acknowledge any other authority."

A call to preach the gospel of Jesus Christ is an unmistakeable experience. It is difficult to explain, but it is somewhat like falling in love with a particular girl whom you want to marry. You may be acquainted with hundreds of girls, but you realize that you love one and want to spend the rest of your life with her. Likewise, you may have several career options, but a call to preach makes you know you want to spend your life in full-time ministry.

As far back as I can trace my family history, on both sides of the family, I find no preachers. Neither my forefathers nor contemporaries had much interest in the church, the Lord, or the preaching of the Word. My family did not determine or influence my vocation—God did! He called me to the ministry. So I feel like Paul when he said, "I thank Christ Jesus our Lord, who hath enabled me, for that he counted me faithful, putting me into the ministry; who was before a blasphemer, and a persecutor, and injurious: but I obtained mercy, because I did it ignorantly in unbelief" (1 Timothy 1:12,13).

I struggled with this call for almost two years. I didn't want to preach. I had other plans for my life. But now I recognize the call of God to preach the gospel as the highest honor that could have come to me. After more than half a century in active ministry, I wouldn't exchange places with the president of the United States or the king of any nation on earth.

A Divine Mission

The minister must have a divine mission. Simply put, that mission is the winning of people to Jesus Christ and nurturing them in the faith. The church and its minister have a specific mission in the world, a specific message for the world: "the ministry of reconciliation . . . the word of reconciliation" (2 Corinthians 5:18,19).

Jesus set forth that mission as preaching and teaching, informing and instructing, propounding and expounding, proclaiming and exclaiming.

The apostle Paul wrote, "[He] gave gifts unto men . . . for the perfecting of the saints, for the work of the ministry, for the edifying of the body of Christ" (Ephesians 4:8-12).

The church is built by winning souls to Christ, and maintained by then training and directing these converts in the service of God to, in turn, win, teach, train, and develop others. The mission of the pastor then is to faithfully proclaim Christ, to faithfully teach Christ in every facet of the program, and to develop and establish every believer by teaching and training him, thus building God's Church.

It is not the minister's mission just to get more members, promote more programs, raise more money, but to lead the people into a consciousness of the presence, power, and purpose of God . . . into an intimate and glorious fellowship.

Realizing that the mission we have been given is the most awesome that a human being could ever have, where are we to receive the ability and the enablement to fulfill this mission?

Some natural abilities will contribute toward success in fulfilling the mission: a good education, a winsome personality, a physical attractiveness, an interest in people, and energy, initiative, determination, drive. Those personal qualities that promote success in the business world are assets in the ministry as well. But human qualities are not the final determiner of success or failure in the work of God.

Acts 3 contains the story of a crippled man sitting at the temple's Gate Beautiful. He was miraculously healed when Peter commanded him to stand up and walk. The man, along with Peter and John, went into the temple shouting and praising God, whereupon the authorities asked Peter and John a very significant question: "By what power, or by what name, have ye done this?" Peter replied: "By the name of Jesus Christ of Nazareth, whom ye crucified, whom God raised from the dead" (Acts 4:7,10).

Just as God empowered and authorized those early preachers, He authorizes and empowers us to accomplish the eternal mission. Jesus Christ is our authority and the Holy Spirit is our power as we endeavor to fulfill our call and accomplish our God-given mission.

A Spiritual Experience

There are two essentials in genuine Christianity: "I have" and "I give," "I possess" and "I share." "I possess"—that is, my experience. "I share"—that is, communicating my experience.

I cannot share something I do not possess. I cannot teach until I have been taught. I cannot impart power until I have received power. I cannot assist others in a right relationship with God until I *have* a right relationship with God.

I believe we who enter the ministry should be able to say, as did Paul, "I was made a minister, according to the gift of the grace of God given unto me by the effectual working of his power . . . that I should preach . . . the unsearchable riches of Christ" (Ephesians 3:7,8).

We are engaged in a spiritual work. It must be done on a spiritual plane by spiritual means. We must use all the modern methods at our disposal to accomplish the eternal purpose, but we must never forget that our success *for* God is in proportion to the power we have *from* God.

In our relationship to God we must be open to Him, sensitive to the leadership of the Holy Spirit, and eager to do God's will with a passion for souls and a genuine love for God and His work.

Unquestionably Obedient

The pastor must be obedient to God without question. The Bible emphasizes that the one condition for the enjoyment of a proper relationship with God is obedience to His authority. Obedience is the very door to salvation. As Paul says, "As by one man's disobedience many were made sinners, so by the obedience of one shall many be made righteous" (Romans 5:19).

Simple faith in Christ brings the forgiveness of sins and starts one on the road to eternal salvation. However, Jesus said, "If ye continue in my word, then are ye my disciples indeed" (John 8:31). Our salvation is in being obedient to God. If we are to have God's blessings and God's best, now and for eternity, we must be obedient to Him.

Genesis 22:18 says that Abraham obeyed God; therefore God said to him, "In thy seed shall all nations of the earth be blessed; because thou hast obeyed my voice." God's blessing was upon Abraham not because he believed God or said he loved God but because he obeyed God. Becoming a channel of blessing can be accomplished only through a submissive will.

The Lord said to Moses concerning Israel, "If ye will obey my voice indeed, . . . ye shall be a peculiar treasure unto me above all people" (Exodus 19:5).

When God spoke to Moses about life in Canaan He said, "I set before you . . . a blessing if you obey . . . and a curse, if you will not obey" (Deuteronomy 11:26,27).

God also said, "If ye be willing and obedient, ye shall eat the good of the land" (Isaiah 1:19). The Bible offers many blessed and wonderful promises to the followers of Jesus Christ—promises of blessings, promises of an abundant life, promises of victory over sin—but all of these promises are conditional, conditional on obedience to God.

Young Saul of Israel stood head and shoulders above his fellowmen, was anointed the first king of Israel, had the Spirit of the Lord upon him, and stood among the prophets of God. He had fellowship with the Lord and guidance and direction from Him, but in time he disobeyed and the Lord said to the prophet Samuel, "It repenteth me that I have set up Saul to be king: for he . . . hath not performed my commandments" (1 Samuel 15:11).

When Saul, in disobedience to the command of God, kept some of the cattle and sheep alive, he tried to explain to Samuel that the people had done so in order to sacrifice them to God. But the Lord said to Saul through Samuel, "To obey is better than sacrifice" (1 Samuel 15:22). Regardless of what good works we do, sacrifices we make, rituals of worship we practice, or acclaim we voice to our Lord, we cannot expect to have God's blessings until we are obedient to Him.

God said to King Saul, "Because thou hast rejected the word of the Lord, he hath also rejected thee" (1 Samuel 15:23). The road to blessing and victory and success in the work of God is marked obedience.

How many preachers today once stood, like Saul, head and shoulders above their fellow preachers, stood among the prophets of the Lord with the Spirit of the Lord upon them, but because of their continued disobedience to God, they disqualified themselves for effective service. They failed to note the apostle Paul's example: "I keep under my body, and bring it into subjection: lest that by any means, when I have preached to others, I myself should be a castaway" (1 Corinthians 9:27).

The Spirit-filled life and ministry are entered through obedience to God. "The Holy Spirit . . . is God's gift to those who obey him" (Acts 5:32, TEV). The outpouring of the Holy Spirit was received by obedience. Jesus commanded His disciples to tarry in the city of Jerusalem until they be endued with power from on high. This command He gave to some five hundred just before He ascended to heaven. Out of that number only one hundred twenty obeyed Him and went to the Upper Room to wait for the infilling of the Holy Spirit. Those who obeyed Him received the gift of the Holy Spirit. Obedience is indeed the door to the Spirit-filled life.

I recall James Blackwood, a member of the famous Blackwood Brothers Gospel Quartet, and a member of First Assembly, coming into my office one day and saying to me, "Pastor, I am so hungry for the fullness of the Holy Spirit." I said to him, "James, do you mean you have not yet received the infilling of the Holy Spirit?" Whereupon he told me that his father and mother, two brothers, and his sister all had been baptized in the Holy Spirit. Since he was a child, he had periodically sought the Lord for the fullness of the Spirit, but had not as yet been baptized in the Spirit.

I said to him, "God wants to fill you with the Holy Spirit, and you most certainly need the fullness of the Spirit, particularly in your work." He said, "Pastor, I am so very, very hungry for the Holy Spirit that I'll do—" He almost said, I'll do anything, then added, "But I will not say 'glory, glory, glory' as I have seen some people do in the past." I explained to him that there is no magic word or special formula or particular ritual through which one must go to receive the Holy Spirit, that the Holy Spirit is a gift and will be poured out upon those whose hearts are prepared and who obey the Lord. I said, "James, you, however, will probably have to say 'glory, glory, glory' before receiving the Holy Spirit because God demands that we be obedient."

James Blackwood left my office frustrated and exceedingly hungry for the fullness of the Holy Spirit. That night the quartet left on a tour of several cities. While traveling down the highway, James was lying in his bunk on the big bus reading a book on the Holy Spirit when he became even more hungry for God's fullness. He eventually said to the Lord, "Oh! God, I am so hungry for the Holy Spirit. I am so anxious to be filled with the Spirit, I'll do anything. I'll even say 'glory, glory, glory' "—and while shouting "glory, glory, glory," he was marvelously baptized in the Holy Spirit. It turned his entire life and ministry around.

It was prophesied of Jesus: "I delight to do thy will, O God." Jesus said of himself, "My meat is to do the will of him that sent me" (John 4:34). "I seek not mine own will, but the will of the Father which hath sent me" (John 5:30). Jesus lived for that one purpose. The controlling power in the life of our Lord was submission. He lived for one purpose—to do the will of God.

Jesus wanted the same motivation to move His disciples, "You are my friends if you do what I command you" (John 15:14, NIV). Friendship with Jesus, that intimate walk with Him, is dependent upon doing whatever He commands.

Jesus said in John 15:15, "Henceforth I call you not servants; for the servant knoweth not what his lord doeth: but I have called you friends; for all things that I have heard of my Father I have made known unto you."

Jesus is saying, in effect, "As a servant, you are redeemed, but as a friend I share with you all those things that God the Father has made known to me. I take you into my confidence. I walk with you and fellowship with you, talk with you and confide in you."

The pastor who wants to be Spirit-filled and have Jesus share insights from the Father must be sensitive and obedient to the will of God.

Attentive to the Holy Spirit

A beautiful example in the New Testament church of one who was sensitive and obedient to the Holy Spirit is Philip. Philip was a man of honest report, full of the Holy Ghost, full of wisdom, and full of faith.

In Acts 8 we have a record of Philip's ministry. Philip was in touch with the Holy Spirit. Not simply given new life by the Spirit of God, he was enabled by the Spirit to express that life cleanly and courageously.

Philip was open about how he might be led by the Spirit. This is tremendously important. We so easily develop certain rigid ideas about the Spirit-guided and Spirit-controlled life. We suppose that because the Spirit dealt with us a certain way one time, He is under obligation to deal with us the same way the next time. This is not so.

Philip was led by the circumstances of persecution to leave Jerusalem and go to Samaria. That is, the Holy Spirit employed the pressure of persecution to lead him out from Jerusalem to the wider ministry that was to be his in Samaria and elsewhere.

Acts 8 describes the great persecution that came to the Church in Jerusalem and the scattering of the disciples throughout the region. "Now those who were scattered went about preaching the word. Philip went down to a city of Samaria" (Acts 8:4, RSV). The Holy Spirit was guiding through circumstance, in this case, the circumstance of persecution.

On another occasion, Philip was led by the ministry of an angel. Right in the midst of his immensely successful revival in Samaria, where signs and wonders and miracles were wrought, the sick being healed and great joy filling the city, verse 26 tells us "an angel of the Lord said to Philip, 'Rise and go toward the south to the road that goes down from Jerusalem to Gaza' " (Acts 8:26, RSV). Here was an extraordinary thing: An angel of God to lead His servant.

But Philip later was led by an inner voice, the direct subjective voice of the Holy Spirit: "The Spirit said to Philip, 'Go up and join this chariot.' So Philip ran to him" (Acts 8:29, RSV). This was an inner speaking of the Holy Spirit to Philip regarding the Ethiopian eunuch whom he was to lead to Christ.

Philip was in touch with the Holy Spirit. He was obedient to God whether it was through circumstance or the voice of an angel or the inner voice of the Holy Spirit speaking to him.

Philip was also flexible as to where he would be used by the Holy Spirit. Try to imagine Philip's situation. In Samaria he had had success. The whole city was stirred, masses of people turned to Christ, great joy filled the city—and right at that time the angel of the Lord told him to go into the desert. Philip obeyed.

If God sees fit to use us in what appears to be an important place, where we have been noticed and perhaps commended, let us not be so big and important in our own eyes that we cannot serve God joyously in some little sphere. If God has blessed us in dealing with great crowds, then let us not be so important in our own thinking that we cannot deal with small crowds or even with one individual.

A missionary from India tells how he was on furlough in Toronto, Canada, during Billy Graham's big campaign there. He was going through some severe trials. He had met Graham only briefly; he wanted to talk with him. But he felt that this preacher who talks with presidents and kings would be too busy.

At one of the meetings, he happened to be at the exit used by Graham. Although he was in the company of colleagues, Dr. Graham saw the missionary, called him by name, and said, "Come with me and let's talk a few minutes." They went to the hotel for a quiet talk, and the missionary later remarked that only God knows what that conversation meant to him.

The value of it lay not only in the counsel Billy Graham gave, but quite as much in the act itself: the turning aside from a thronged auditorium for one lonely, perplexed missionary. This is being open about where we are to be used.

More and more, I am convinced that possibly the most effective ministry is person-to-person. We must never forget that we do not minister to masses, we minister to individuals. The individuals make up the masses.

Some years ago I was sitting in a meeting of the General Presbytery, the legislative body of the Assemblies of God when the General Council is not in session. Looking around the room I saw three men, two of them district superintendents and one a district secretary, who had been brought to Jesus Christ under my ministry. Sitting there I said to myself, "I wonder what sermon I preached when so-and-so was converted." Upon further reflection, I remembered that all three of these men were won to Jesus Christ not by my sermons, but my personal conversation, witnessing and counseling with them.

Philip was in touch with the gospel. Not a theologian like Paul or an apostle like Peter, he nonetheless had a firm grasp of the essentials of the gospel.

The gospel is not what men think about God, or what they do to make themselves acceptable to God. This is religion, not the gospel. The gospel is what God has done for us. It is God breaking into history with His virgin born Son taking your sins and mine and making an atonement for them by the blood of His cross, then sealing that victory over sin, death, and the devil by His mighty resurrection. That is the message Philip preached to the Samaritans.

Philip was in touch with the people. If Philip had not loved people with an affection that only Christ could give to him, do you think he would have gone to Samaria? The woman of Samaria said to Jesus, "How is it that you, a Jew, ask a drink of me, a woman of Samaria?" (John 4:9, RSV).

The Samaritans were a mixed race; the Jews despised them. And the Samaritans resented the Jews. Nevertheless, it was to the city of Samaria that Philip went and proclaimed Christ.

The Ethiopian was a Gentile, even worse than the Samaritans in the eyes of the Jews. But Calvary's love had stripped Philip of all racial haughtiness and hostility. He joined himself to the Ethiopian's chariot.

If we as ministers are to have any measure of success, we must be sensitive and obedient to the leadership of the Holy Spirit. We cannot always explain it or define it, but we can know it.

In fifty-five years of active ministry, I have pastored five churches. Four of the five churches I did not want to pastor at the time I accepted the call to do so. But in each case I felt definitely led to accept the pastorate, knowing in my heart God was speaking to me about the matter.

The church I wanted asked me if I would consider the pastorate, and I replied in the affirmative. I hoped the congregation would elect me. They did. But when I look back over that ministry, I accomplished perhaps less of eternal value in that pastorate than in any of the other four. In the other four churches I was able to lead the congregations into new buildings and programs, and to accept innovations that I believe will count for eternity.

Even when the Memphis church extended an invitation, I did not want to accept. I was only 31 years of age; my wife and I were on the evangelistic field. We were having the greatest and apparently most successful ministry in our lives. We were receiving calls from the largest churches all across the nation, and invitations to speak in camp meetings, conferences, and conventions. We were extremely happy in this work. Then came the invitation to Memphis. The church was poorly located, small (about one hundred people), and discouraged. But God laid that congregation and city on my heart. And I obeyed. The greatest years of my ministry and the most enjoyable years of my life followed.

Total Commitment to God and the Ministry

Total commitment means the act or process of entrusting or consigning or pledging one's self completely to a person or a cause.

I am convinced that the chief ingredient for success in the ministry is commitment. The chief factor in church growth, both spiritually and numerically, is commitment. Without commitment on the part of pastors and people, little or no growth can occur, numerically— or spiritually.

The Bible and church history records indicate that people have never experienced spiritual growth apart from a commitment to God and His will. Commitment is a fact. We are all committed to something. All of us are ruled by something—something good, or something bad, or something less than the best.

When the late Glen Frank, president of the University of Wisconsin, analyzed our national life, he said, "There is business with its passion for profits, there is politics with its passion for power, and there is society with its passion for pleasure."

But a person arrives at the superlative when he comes to terms with God, when he develops a passion for Him. The crisis of self-surrender has been the turning point in the life of those who have really come to know Jesus Christ in His fullness and have given themselves to the call of God.

Take a look at Christian history and you will discover that the people who made a mark for God and for good in the world were those whose commitment was unlimited, who brought themselves, their will, their actions, into submission to God.

As long as I have been a Christian, the attitude of some professing Christians has disturbed me. Their attitude is one of escapism. It is reflected in their songs, testimonies, and sermons. Most of their songs are about heaven, a "pie in the sky" religion.

I believe in the beauties, the glories, and the blessings of the future life. I look forward to eternity with my Lord and the saints in heaven. But until that time comes, I believe that the key word is not *escape* but *encounter*—for the individual Christian, the church, and especially the minister.

The prayer of every Christian should be, "Thy Kingdom come, thy will be done on earth as in heaven" instead of "Oh! for the wings of a dove for then I would fly away and be at rest." Few words or acts are more important to the life and ministry of the pastor than the word *commit* and the act of commitment.

It is exceedingly important for every member of the church to be involved in the work and ministry of the church. Church activities are not for spectators but participators.

However, one can be a member of the church, enjoy its ministry and use the services it provides (such as its prayers, sympathy, love and concern in time of sickness or a death in the family) and still not be committed to the church. One can even be involved in certain activities in the church and still not be committed to the church and the cause for which it really stands.

It is also possible for a pastor to be involved in the ministry, to be involved in the work of the Lord, but not committed. Commitment, at times, requires sacrifice, requires one hundred percent effort, requires courage, faith, and determination. What we need more than involvement, as important as that is, is commitment.

The difference between involvement and commitment is illustrated by the story of the hen and the pig. Standing beside the road one morning, they saw the people on a hunger march pass, en route to Washington to protest their lot in life. The hen said to the pig, "I feel sorry for those people." The pig replied, "So do I." The hen then said, "I wish that we could do something for them." Whereupon the pig replied, "I am certainly willing to do anything that I can." The hen suggested, "Let us provide a good breakfast of ham and eggs for them." Now, for the hen that was involvement—but for the pig, it meant total commitment.

I had only one brother, some three years younger than I. As small boys, we lived in a rural area and spent much time roaming the woods and fields—just the two of us. I recall with amusement some of the little pranks I used to play on him. For example, we might come to a small brook when I would say to him, "Vernon, I don't believe you can jump that brook." And he would say with gusto, "Of course I can jump that little brook." And after some friendly arguing as to whether or not he was physically able to leap over that brook, he would back away and start his run toward the little body of water. Just as he would get to the brink of the stream I would shout, "No! No! Don't do it!" He would hesitate just a moment. And we all know he who hesitates gets wet when jumping a stream of water. He was not fully committed to the task, or my interruption would not have broken his concentration. If we are totally committed, we can ignore interruptions and achieve our purpose.

Esther was totally committed. Remember how Haman plotted to kill all the Jews and Mordecai prevailed upon Esther to go to the king on their behalf? After some soul searching, Esther made a complete commitment by saying she would approach the king: it might mean her death. Nevertheless she said, "If I perish, I perish."

This is the same kind of total commitment that Patrick Henry made when he said, "I do not know what course others may take, but as for me give me liberty or give me death."

J. W. Tucker made that commitment when he returned in 1964 to the Congo. Knowing the great danger that beset his mission, but with the love of God and love for the people, he went nevertheless, saying, like Paul of old, "the love of God constraineth us." It cost J. W. Tucker his life.

Total commitment means putting God first. It means that the will of God is paramount regardless of the consequences. The apostle Paul said, "This one thing I do." And Jesus declared, "For this purpose came I into the world."

To fulfill our commitment to God, we must break through the barrier of indifference, worldliness, pride. We must break through every obstacle that hinders us in our service to God. We must break through the materialistic spirit that prevails today, the fog and haze of this world, and realize again that we are not our own, but we are bought with a price; that we have a high and holy calling. We must break through the principalities and powers to real spiritual life, to consecrate fully our time, our talent, our treasure, to God and His church.

In 1955, I had been in full-time ministry about twenty-five years when I had an opportunity to make a large sum of money. I grew up fatherless and very poor, but I had always believed that I could make money if I devoted my time and effort in that direction. Now apparently that opportunity had come. It would mean giving up my pastorate and an active ministry. But I rationalized that I would still be available to preach on weekends and special occasions, that I would give to the Lord not ten percent but twenty-five percent of all this money I was going to make—possibly more. I also rationalized that after twenty-five years in the ministry (much of it in very difficult situations and without much material benefit) that I had made my contribution to full-time preaching.

I was giving very serious consideration to this business proposition when a polyp developed on my vocal chords, creating constant hoarseness. I was on radio every day and television every week, besides the responsibilities of preaching in my pulpit on Sundays and Wednesdays. Speaking became very difficult and embarrassing. I consulted five doctors before the real difficulty was discovered.

Some physicians indicated that it might be a malignancy. I was faced with the possibility of not being able to talk again or to preach the gospel. It was then that I realized what a glorious and wonderful privilege I had to simply preach the unsearchable riches of Jesus Christ. I made a new commitment to God, regardless of the cost, to preach Christ as long as I was physically able to speak His name. My happiest years of ministry have been since that day!

Before he was killed in an Ecuadorian jungle by the Auca Indians, Jim Elliot had written, "He is no fool who gives what he cannot keep to gain what he cannot lose."

If we really want to be successful ministers, if we want to count for God and for eternity, if we want to fulfill God's eternal purpose and plan for our lives, if we want to be able to join the apostle Paul in saying, "I have fought a good fight, I have kept the faith, now there is a crown of righteousness laid up for me," then we must start with God and stay with God.

2

The Pastor and His Family

The pastor is a unique man, divinely called, ordained, and commissioned to preach the gospel, to lead God's people in worship, in evangelism, in building the church. He deals with human souls; he makes eternal decisions; he admonishes and counsels the congregation on matters of utmost importance. Yet none of these is more important than his responsibility as husband to his wife and father to his children.

The pastor's home should be a spiritual home. Just as he projects an image in the church and in the community as a man of God, he should project that same image in his home. His family should think of him not only as husband or father, but also as one who is fully committed to God and the ministry. He does not have to have a pontifical attitude to be spiritual, but he must be consistent—the same man in the home that he is in the pulpit.

The parsonage should be a house of prayer and praise, a place where the Bible is read and taught, and a place where the family members manifest the fruit of the Spirit (Galatians 5:22,23). The pastor's home should provide the kind of atmosphere in which the Christian graces thrive.

Atmosphere of the Home

Human beings in any close-knit relationship have interests and sentiments, creating that indefinable something that we call atmosphere. Let us call it emotional weather. Since the home is that form of social community in which the participants are parents and children, each family is bound to create its own emotional weather depending on the dominant ideals, sentiments, and interests that are found there. More and more we are coming to realize the subtle power of atmosphere in the family and elsewhere.

Dr. Jacob Norman, a psychiatric counselor, insists that education for marriage should begin at three or four years of age. He claims that it is not so much a matter of telling the child the so-called facts of life as it is of having the child unconsciously pick up the proper attitudes toward love, sex, and marriage in his daily homelife. Values and attitudes should be guided to a lesser degree in school and in the outside world. Thus the atmosphere of the home is the main influence in developing these attitudes.

That is true about many issues of life. We develop an emotional slant toward them before we are aware of it. It comes to us by absorption, so to speak. What we get by direct instruction may have value, but what we get by absorption has power. What is preached at us may or may not stick, but what is kindled within us, what we absorb, is almost certain to endure.

Thomas Paine, the brilliant infidel-patriot, said, "I was an infidel before I was 5 years old." What did he mean? All that he may have meant I do not know, but one thing is clear, the emotional atmosphere of his childhood home was anything but conducive to the love of God.

On the other hand, good emotional weather drives young lives toward the harbors of happiness and ports of peace. Dr. G. Campbell Morgan, the world-renowned Scottish preacher of the first half of this century, had sons who were preachers. Once his daughter was asked, "Who is the greatest preacher in your family?" She replied, "The greatest preacher in our family is Mother." She was not saying that Mrs. Morgan was always lecturing and scolding. She simply meant that her mother's Christian spirit, the firmness of her faith, the purity of her love, the strength of her courage and her patience, created an emotional weather in which powerful spiritual results were realized. The Morgan home was truly Christian. Its atmosphere was healthy for the development of Christian graces and character.

Precept, Example, Discipline

The pastor as a father must teach his children by precept, by example, and by discipline. God gave a specific commandment concerning teaching our children His precepts. "Thou shalt teach them diligently unto thy children and shalt talk of them when thou sittest in thine house, and when thou walkest by the way, and when thou liest down, and when thou risest up" (Deuteronomy 6:7). Solomon said, "Train up a child in the way he should go: and when he is old he will not depart from it" (Proverbs 22:6).

Parents are responsible to teach and train their children in the ways of God. Children must be taught at home. Authorities have said that by age ten a child learns more than half of all that he will ever know. This being true, then, we must teach our young children the things of God.

God's Word says, in effect, "We must learn piety first at home." It was the English evangelist "Gipsy" Smith who said, "You save an old man and you save a unit; but save a boy, and you save a multiplication table."

Parents, particularly pastors, should never take their children's salvation for granted. When children are born into a Christian home, live in a Christian atmosphere, go to the church services several times a week, and participate in almost all the activities involving the church, it is very easy to assume, almost unconsciously, that the child is a Christian. We must never forget that salvation is a personal matter and no one, whatever environment he may live in, whatever he may have been taught, whatever examples may have been set before him, can know God and the forgiveness of his sins unless he himself believes in the Lord Jesus Christ.

Children need academic teaching. They need regular and faithful instruction in the things of God, but no lesson is better taught than by example. Parents do teach by example, either good or bad.

These days it is greatly emphasized that fathers should spend a great deal of time with their children. That is sound. Fathers need to spend as much time as possible with their children, especially their sons.

In looking back over more than a half-century of active ministry, one of my greatest regrets is that I did not spend more time with my boys during the time they were growing up. By the grace of God, and through His tender mercies, both are Christians. But as I look back now, if those years could be relived, I would spend more time with my boys in their formative years.

However, just spending time with our children does not automatically provide the proper example. We must show them the proper example, living before them the way we would want them to live before God.

Not only should the pastor teach his children by precept and by example, but by discipline. No person has ever been well-trained who has not learned discipline. Parents are doing their children no favors by neglecting their discipline. It is our responsibility to rear children to face life as it really is.

I once had a professor of psychology who constantly emphasized the positive, saying that his children never learned the meaning of the word *no* until they heard it from the neighbor's children. This prompted me to ask him, "Is it possible for any person to develop a normal personality and become a person of character without learning to say no when it is necessary?"

Permissive child psychology, mixed with parental weakness, has led to lawlessness on the part of thousands of young people in America. A child who does not respect the rules of his home will not respect the laws of his country.

God's Word demands that parents discipline their children. The wise man Solomon said, "He that spareth his rod hateth his son: but he that loveth him chasteneth him betimes" (Proverbs 13:24). Solomon also admonished, "Chasten thy son while there is hope, and let not thy soul spare for his crying" (Proverbs 19:18). The wise man also said, "The rod and reproof give wisdom: but a child left to himself bringeth his mother to shame" (Proverbs 29:15).

Such discipline, of course, should be administered not through harshness but through genuine love. Paul wrote specifically to fathers: "Provoke not your children to wrath: but bring them up in the nurture and admonition of the Lord" (Ephesians 6:4).

Paul also emphasized that one of the qualifications for a church leader is, "one that ruleth well his own house, having his children in subjection with all gravity" (1 Timothy 3:4).

In 1 Samuel we have the story of Eli, a man called of God to be priest of Israel. His sons were evil men and corrupt. They were accused of misappropriating the offerings and desecrating the sacrifices made in the temple, as well as being guilty of adultery. This lack of parental discipline brought God's judgment: "For I have told him that I will judge his house forever for the iniquity which he knoweth; because his sons made themselves vile, and he restrained them not" (1 Samuel 3:3).

King David was not a priest or a pastor, but he was a leader and should have been a spiritual leader of his nation and his family. He is a classic example of one who succeeded in leadership but failed as a father.

In many respects, David had been successful. The story of his life reads like a romance. He came up from the ranks, a shepherd lad without too much prestige in his own family. He had a brilliant mind and ready courage. He was attractive, he was alert—and he was equal to almost any occasion. Rapidly he climbed the ladder of success: hero, soldier, king, statesman. He succeeded in welding together the quarreling tribes of Israel. He was financially successful and the people looked back on his reign in Israel as the Golden Age. A success story could easily be written about him called "From a Shepherd's Tent to the King's Palace."

David was, perhaps, Israel's greatest king, but he was a miserable failure as a father. Similarly a pastor can be a great preacher, yet fail as a father.

The only thing that distinguishes the children of David in the Bible is disgrace. Amnon was a rapist; his half-sister Tamar his victim; her brother Absalom her avenger. It was a sordid affair worthy of the example David himself set with Bathsheba.

Second Samuel records the death of Absalom and the emotional reaction of David. Israel was engaged in a civil war initiated by the rebellion of Absalom and his attempt to usurp the throne from his father. David sent word to his general, "Deal gently for my sake with . . . Absalom" (2 Samuel 18:5).

After the army had gone out to battle, a messenger returned with the sad news that Absalom had been killed; David cried out, "O my son Absalom! my son, my son Absalom! I would God I had died for thee, O Absalom, my son, my son!" (2 Samuel 18:33).

The regret in this cry of David seemed to be that he felt his boy had died needlessly. He seemed to be saying that he had lost his boy when he might have saved him—"Had I only been a better father."

David was a busy man. He apparently had little time for his sons. A pastor too struggles under tremendous pressures, the multiplied demands for his time and energy, sometimes shifting the responsibility for the spiritual welfare of his children to their mother. This ought not to be. Whatever our responsibilities as a spiritual leader may be, we cannot, we must not, shift our responsibilities as a father.

People in Christian ministry must be committed to taking care of their children and rearing them properly. They are not someone else's business. Gordon McDonald says as a young pastor he once asked an older preacher, "What is more important, my family or the Lord's work?" The response was, "Gordon, your family *is* the Lord's work."

Little time and a bad example are a deadly combination in discharging the responsibilities of fatherhood. Pastors must be careful to do and to say only those things that will bring glory and honor to God. By example, we most certainly can teach our children the real values of life.

In a pastor's home, there should never be criticism of other Christians. The pastor and his wife should never discuss, with or before the children, difficulties and problems that arise among the people of the congregation. Gossip and criticism of various church members should never be permitted. There should be an earnest effort to build confidence in Christians in the minds of the children.

If the pastor's children lose confidence in the members of their father's church and come to believe that some of the people do not treat their dad right, those children are hindered in making deep commitments to Christ and His church.

This caution regarding gossip should protect not only the local congregation but all Christians. The pastor should do all in his power to build confidence in the church and the clergy worldwide. The minister must protect his children from gossip, criticism, and cynicism about God's people.

This was illustrated to our family forcefully when our youngest son came home on a weekend after enrolling in a Christian college. He said to me, "Dad, why didn't you ever tell me that some churches have difficulties between the pastor and deacons, the pastor and members, and that sometimes pastors are forced to leave their pastorates? And that ministers sometimes have moral problems and lose their credentials?"

There may be a danger in building a wall of protection around our children so high that the shock of reality becomes detrimental. Nevertheless, I still believe that we must do all within our power to maintain the confidence of our children in Christ and His total church.

Other measures should be taken to ensure that such a wall of protection does not isolate the children: "There should be good books to read and wisely selected television programs to watch so that each may exert a positive and broadening cultural influence. The pastor's home should be a place where that which is positive, good, and culturally meaningful can be explored and entered into in a very meaningful way. This, of itself, will create a very positive dimension to the internal dynamics of the pastor's home and will help eliminate the cultural isolation that sometimes characterizes the children of ministers."[1]

The Pastor's Wife

I once heard a very godly wife of a pastor say, "A good wife is the pastor's greatest asset." I am not prepared to go that far, but I must say that the pastor's wife is most certainly one of his greatest assets. A good wife can contribute greatly to the pastor's success, as well as to his personal happiness.

When I look back over more than a half-century of active ministry, I confess that, whatever success I may have had, much of the credit must go to a good, consecrated, and talented wife who shared willingly, sacrificially, joyfully, and faithfully in that ministry.

The pastor's wife, in the natural, often has an almost untenable position with the church. She goes to whatever church the pastor feels led to accept, whether she feels a definite call or not. She, in effect, becomes a servant of the people her husband is pastoring. At times, I suspect, she must feel like wearing a label that says, "I am the property of the church."

The wife often must become a buffer between her husband and members of the church. I recall that sometimes members who did not want to complain to me would unload on my wife all their pent-up feelings about what I should do and what things they disliked.

Sometimes people endeavor to dictate to the pastor's wife how she should rear her children, manage her home, and even what she should wear. I remember when my wife and I were rather young, we were conducting special meetings in one of the larger churches. This was when "toeless" shoes for women first appeared on the market. My wife thought they were so beautiful that she purchased a pair. The first time she wore them, she was told by some of the congregation that a preacher's wife should not dress in such a manner as to expose her toes. It was difficult to understand the inconsistency of that congregation when some of them invited us to a swimming party that weekend.

Mary LaGrand Bouma says, "The women who are married to ministers are usually among the walking wounded. Some are nursing serious injuries, others have received only minor cuts and scrapes which seem to have healed easily without leaving any scars. Few escape completely unscathed.

"Pastor's wives, like their husbands, suffer from discouragement. For one thing they and their children, like their husbands, are right up there in the public eye . . . on display. They are almost always introduced to others as 'pastors wives.' " One pastor's wife remarked that no one says, "This is Janie, our plumber's wife," or "our lawyer's wife," but the pastor's wife is invariably presented as "our minister's wife."[2]

The pastor's wife, so often, struggles with the small amount of money she has for feeding, clothing, and caring for the family. Although the situation seems to be improving in this area, money problems are still a reality for a large proportion of pastors and their wives. "A pamphlet put out by the U.S. Department of Labor that lists occupations from the highest paid on down reveals that out of 432 occupations listed, clergymen ranked 317th . . . (they) rank with the lowest-paying occupations and with unskilled labor. . . . Though they rank next to the bottom economically, educationally they rank with the top earning occupations—lawyers, physicians, dentists, judges, college professors, scientists, engineers, and managers.

"The minister's wives are the ones who must do most of the coping with the financial problems. They must make do or do without. A strange thing is that the minister is completely surrounded by affluence these days, in which he cannot share. He is a professional man and often his friends are those in the professions who are making much more money than he does. The minister and his wife cannot afford a life-style similar to that of their friends.

"The frequent moves which a pastor's family must make are another problem for many of the wives. Living in a parsonage is one aspect of the ministerial life that is often difficult for the pastor's wife. In some places, and some times, members of the congregation think they can come over to the parsonage whenever they please because, after all, it belongs to them. This problem seems to be most acute in the cases where the furnishings of the house are a part of the parsonage and do not belong to the pastor. In many places, churches are now providing a house allowance for the pastor that enables the minister to rent or purchase his own home."[3]

The pastor's wife has no one in the local congregation in whom she can confide. A good pastor and his wife can never have close friends (the kind you confide in) in their church. This is very difficult for women, because they usually want that kind of friendship. All of us, as a matter of fact, enjoy being with some people more than others. But to really succeed as a good pastor, one must be the same to all the people, the good and bad, rich and poor, intelligent and ignorant, young and old.

"In one church, the pastor and his wife became very involved with another couple. They would go out together every week. They were so close they excluded and neglected others in the church. It caused jealousy and resentment, and eventually the problem became so intense it caused the pastor and his wife to leave the church.

"Some wives are manipulated by those whom they consider their close friends. One pastor's wife says, 'Not long after we had come to the church I formed a great friendship. Something inside me said not to get too close, but I was hungry for a close friend, so I did anyway. We talked a lot; she knew when someone in the church offended me, and she knew my personal feelings about the church. Later we had a split in the church and she went with the other side. She betrayed *all* my confidences. Only if you experience this personally can you imagine the pain it brings.' "[4]

The pastor's wife is a public person. Whether she wants it or not, her life and that of her family are almost an open book. Many pastor's wives, no doubt, would like to have more privacy and be able to separate their personal lives from the ministry and to spend more time with their husband and children.

Be that as it may, the pastor may still fail to have a happy and warm relationship with his own wife, even though he is successful at helping other people solve their relationship problems.

Ralph M. Smucker points out ten problems in the relationship of the pastor and his wife:

1. The pastor is likely to have a strong, aggressive personality.

He is more used to creating and promoting ideas and programs than to accepting and implementing the ideas of others.

2. The pastor is deeply committed to his work and gives it his best time and energy. Other responsibilities tend to take second, third, or even fourth place in his scheme of priorities.

3. The pastor is constantly giving his attention and energy to others. He may separate his work from his wife to the point that he does not discuss church matters with her at all. This reduces her sense of worth and contribution to his pastoral ministry.

4. The pastor's time is not his own, or at least it seems that way. He is often absent from home and his income hardly permits him to offer his family the compensation of conveniences that make family living easier.

5. The pastor and his family live a fishbowl existence in which the normal problems of family life tend to be magnified.

6. The pastor's wife has no pastor besides her husband. (She lives with him six days and then must believe that God speaks to him on the seventh.)

7. Tension may arise because the pastor's wife observes his unending patience with others, but seeks in vain for the same patience in his dealing with those in his own home.

8. The pastor spends a good deal of time with couples who are having problems and his wife may sometimes fear that the women he counsels are transferring their affection to him.

9. The pastor is in the spotlight most of the time. He receives spiritual, emotional, and material rewards as he carries out his work. His sense of fulfillment may be much greater than his wife's because of his firsthand experience in witnessing the blessings of God and the results of his labors. If she receives a full diet of his problems, the criticisms, the doubts, and the unresolved questions, she may feel unhappy and frustrated because she seems unable to do anything.

10. Men who make good pastors usually choose to marry women with strong and sensitive personalities, having conviction and enthusiasm. Unless there is a continual effort to build bridges between these two strong personalities, a great gulf may develop.[5]

Dr. Guynes says, "The ministry is not an easy road, and it requires singleness of heart and purpose. Contradiction between the minister and his wife in the work of the Lord brings problems that sometimes are beyond human capacity to handle. More often than not the results are either a very ineffective ministry or the abandonment of the ministry entirely."[6]

This points up unmistakably that each individual who feels a call of God on his life for full-time ministry should give consideration to matrimony only in the light of that divine call. He most certainly should not become unequally yoked together with one who does not share his commitment to the ministry.

The young preacher should seek a companion whose life is as open to the things of God as his own, one whose desire is to do the will of God and to work in God's harvest field. He should be careful to select one who is not domineering in her personality, one who can take a secondary role in the public relationships in which the pastor is involved, but also one who can take individual initiative in those areas where the home and ministry require it.

Lucille Lavender in her book *They Cry, Too!* states, " 'Among the professions, the clergy rank third in the number of divorces granted each year.' Public life and service is accompanied with unique marital stress and strain. Often the non-public partner suffers silently until, as one pastor's wife put it, 'the worm turns.' "[7]

Despite the struggles, sacrifices, and restrictions required in being a minister's wife, according to a poll published in *Leadership*, most women are happy in their roles. Ninety percent of those surveyed said they enjoyed being a pastor's wife. "In fact, eighty-five percent said under no circumstance would they want their husbands to change professions. Granted, there are problems unique to the calling; but the wives said, in effect, that the problems are outweighed by the joys."

Many pastors' wives express their feelings in this manner: " 'I love being a pastor's wife. I feel fulfilled in this way of life.' " Another said, " 'I feel privileged to be a pastor's wife, and I enjoy the consideration I receive. I have had an influence with parishioners that I never would have had as a lay person.' " One wife wrote, " 'I am much more involved in my husband's work than I would be in any other type of job; I go with him to his job. Sundays I go with him to work, and I do things with him, which, if he were working somewhere else I wouldn't be able to do. The fact that I am with him on part of the job ensures that *I'll* be more involved in the ministry.' " There are other similar expressions, for example, " 'When you share your husband's ministry on the front lines, you lead people to the love of Christ. In this way, I see that this is a calling from God, not just a job.' 'It's given me a chance to grow, mature, learn, love, share in lives, and be involved in a wide range of experiences. I have enjoyed it to the fullest.' "[8]

The Pastor's Children

The pastor's family lives in a fishbowl. Unrealistic expectations of the behavior of the pastor's children create unfair pressures. Many people expect instant maturity of the children and don't give them a chance to go through the process of growing up. When the child realizes that he or she cannot maintain the expected life-style of perfection, scars are left.

Someone said, "Preachers' kids can't win. If we are good, it is no virtue. Whatever we do right, we have been trained or forced to do. Whatever we believe, we were taught to believe."

Delmar Guynes writes, "A 'fishbowl' experience has caused some ministers' children to react negatively to the ministry because they were constantly under observation by the people to whom their father ministered. The pastor should look on his children as normal human beings whose needs require attention as much as those of the children of his parishioners.

"It is not uncommon for churchfolk to feel the pastor's children ought to be somewhat special and behave themselves better than other children. The pastor should project an attitude toward his children and his congregation that will reduce this kind of emphasis. Certainly the pastor's home, including his children, is to be exemplary, but to allow this to be overemphasized can produce such negative reactions that the pastor's children will have little interest or concern about spiritual things and the role of the church."[9]

I think it is generally agreed that the advantages of being a preacher's kid far outweigh the disadvantages. One "P.K." wrote, "We have had people in our home other children have never had the benefit of knowing: African pastors, foreign missionaries, evangelists, other preachers. We were able to talk with them, play games with them, and find out more about the world and what makes people tick."

A parent said, "Our children have seen areas of this country and met new people in different cultures they never would have had the opportunity to know if they were not P.K.s." Another testified, "My daughter spent two summers when she was a teenager with the youth mission group. They saw two hundred children won to Christ. It was exciting and satisfying to watch her grow in relationship to God. That is worth any disadvantage that might come with being in the ministry."[10]

Dr. Guynes states, "The minister's children, under normal circumstances, hold a greater potential for ministry involvement than those not reared in the parsonage. They build on the foundation of their parents' ministerial experience and do not have to start at the zero level like those who have not had such an advantage. This potential for ministry is not automatic, nor does it in any way replace the need for a divine call and those spiritual qualifications that must come uniquely to each individual.

"Aside from ministerial potential, it will usually be true that the children of ministers hold high levels of potential for many other kinds of meaningful involvement. This has been apparent in that throughout the years, children from ministers' homes have gone into worthy professions in which they have served with distinction."[11]

Years ago I read in a well-known magazine that over a period of years the children of ministers were more successful than children of any other classification of parents, such as lawyers, doctors, business executives, and the like.

This is believed to be true in part because of the character of the parents, their example, the training they gave to their children, and the environment in which they were brought up. This also may be due to the minister's orientation to intellectual study and to good human relationships in the church, in the home, and in the community.

This can be illustrated in the family trees of two men who lived at the same time, in the same part of the country—one an irreligionist and the other a clergyman.

Max Jukes lived a godless life during the early part of the eighteenth century. Twelve hundred of his descendants were traced. He married an ungodly girl and from their descendants three hundred and ten died as paupers, one hundred and thirty were criminals, seven were murderers, and fifty of the women lived lives of "notorious debauchary." The descendants cost the state one and a quarter million dollars.

Jonathan Edwards, the great preacher and man of God, was a contemporary of Max Jukes. He married a godly girl. An investigation of more than fourteen hundred descendants revealed thirteen college presidents, more than one hundred college professors, three United States senators, thirty judges, more than one hundred lawyers, sixty doctors, seventy-five army and navy officers, more than one hundred preachers and missionaries, sixty authors and editors of prominence, one vice president of the United States, more than eighty public officials in other capacities, and two hundred and eighty-five college graduates (among whom were governors and diplomats). His descendants did not cost the state one single dollar![12]

"The home is never the *last* place to live the Christian life; it is always the *first* place."[13]

The pastor's family is the most influential family in the church, and often in the community. The pastor's family is an example either for good or for less than good! The pastor's family unfortunately live in a "fishbowl" and their activities are known and often widely discussed by the congregation and the community.

The pastor and his family should represent the ideal for the Christian community. Pastors and their families are, in fact, "epistles known and read of all men" and thus should "walk circumspectly before all men."

NOTES

[1]Thomas F. Zimmerman, ed., *And He Gave Pastors* (Springfield, MO: Gospel Publishing House, 1979), p. 110.

[2]Mary LaGrand Bouma, "Ministers' Wives: The Walking Wounded," *Leadership* 1 (Winter 1980):63.

[3]Ibid., pp. 67, 68, 69.

[4]Pat Valeriano, "A Survey of Ministers' Wives," *Leadership* 2 (Fall 1981):67.

[5]Ralph M. Smucker, "The Minister and His Wife," *Christianity Today*, June 20, 1969, pp. 3-4.

[6]Zimmerman, p. 115.

[7]LaGrand Bouma, p. 63.

[8]Valeriano, pp. 64, 65, 66.

[9]Zimmerman, pp. 120, 121.

[10]Valeriano, p. 66.

[11]Zimmerman, p. 121.

[12]A. E. Winship, *Jukes—Edwards* (Harrisburg, PA: R. L. Myers & Co., 1900).

[13]J. D. Middlebrook and Larry Summers, *The Church and Family* (Springfield, MO: Gospel Publishing House, 1980), p. 11.

3

The Pastor and His Staff

A church that maintains a staff of full-time, paid employees usually has personnel in the clerical and secretarial area and in the maintenance/custodial area, with the custodial personnel employed on an hourly basis.

The pastoral and professional staff is composed of ministers and lay directors who are assigned specific responsibilities as spelled out in a job description. This chapter is about that group.

However energetic and efficient a pastor may be, he can do only so much. When the church reaches a certain size, it is necessary that assistance be obtained, usually in some type of specialized ministry, such as music, Christian education, youth, and business administration.

God can and does call people to specialized ministries. Their contribution to the advancement of the cause of Christ is exceedingly important. In light of this fact, some people who are especially gifted, for example, in the areas of music, education, visitation, counseling, and administration, should give serious consideration to making it a lifetime work. People who have qualifications in specialized ministries can find a rich and satisfying ministry. Not every person is called to or qualified for the responsibility of pastoring a church.

It is a mistake for many Christian workers to believe that these specialized ministries are only stepping stones to what is commonly called a full-time preaching ministry. In fact, it is advantageous for the young preacher who expects to be a full-time pastor or missionary to spend some years in an assistant pastor role. Such an apprenticeship will provide valuable experience before he assumes the tremendous responsibilities of pastoring.

Selecting Staff Members

The pastor, church board, and congregation must decide when additional staff is needed. Some churches require more assistance than others because of the many functions, ministries, and services the church provides for the congregation, community, and general public.

There are several classifications of staff personnel: associate pastor, assistant pastor, assistant to the pastor, business administrator, directors of Christian education, youth, children, music, visitation, pastoral care, and bus ministries.

The selection of a staff member should be determined by the greatest need in the church. For example, on the surface, music, Christian education, and youth might be areas of equal consideration for paid staffing. However, if a layman is qualified to direct music, and the pastor has training in Christian education, perhaps youth represents the greatest staff need.

The choosing of associates and staff members is of paramount importance. All staff members should be appointed by the pastor! The pastor may want advice and counsel of the church board on such matters, but the final selection of all paid personnel should be the prerogative of the pastor. This will assure his control of those who must work under his supervision and for whom he must be responsible.

All staff members and all other personnel, including assistants, business administrator, secretaries, and custodians, should be responsible to the pastor—who in the final analysis is responsible to God and the congregation for the success of the church. Such an arrangement will assure a smoother operation of the total church.

The pastor should never select a staff member just because he needs assistance or because so-and-so is a very nice young man and needs a job.

Assistants should be chosen (1) because the church has a specific need/task and (2) someone qualified by training, aptitude, and attitude has been found to fill that position.

Finding the right person for the right position should not be left to chance. Securing complete resumes, contacting references, interviewing the candidate, and evaluating your findings must take place before you can intelligently choose a staff person. The answer to staff motivation is to hire the right people in the first place.

Compensation and Working Conditions

Compensation and working conditions should be stated very clearly and understood by both the senior pastor and the staff member at the time the new staff member assumes his responsibilities. Perhaps the best procedure in handling such matters is for the church board or congregation (whoever has such authority) to approve the employing of a person for such a position. The board could set a salary and fringe benefits for the position, but leave the choice of the individual to the senior pastor.

Some boards of churches having multiple staff set the salary by classification, paying so much, for example, to a music director, so much to a business administrator, and so much to the associate or assistant pastor. Others set a maximum for these and other positions, and the pastor negotiates the exact amount to be paid to the individual.

However the staff member's compensation is arrived at, he should be given a clear understanding of what he is to receive in salary and benefits (if any), such as life insurance, hospitalization, pension plan, sick leave, emergency leave, vacation, automobile expenses, housing allowance, and (if the staff member is a layperson) social security.

When churches pay all moving expenses for a pastor or staff member (running into hundreds or thousands of dollars) that investment needs to be protected. First Assembly had the following provision listed in its operational manual, which applied to all personnel:

> The church shall advance all costs for moving the household goods of a professional staff member to Memphis and charge it to his account for a three-year period. In the event that staff member decides to terminate before the end of the first three-year period, the balance will be charged back to his account per one-third of the total amount per year. (Example: after one year, the staff member shall reimburse the church two-thirds of the original amount; two years, one-third of the original amount will be the balance, after three years no reimbursement will be necessary.) If the church terminates the employee the reimbursement clause will be negotiated.

In most cases, staff members in a church in the beginning of their tenure are young. Many just out of Bible college desire to further their education by attending school part-time in pursuit of a master's degree or a doctorate. The class time and study can be at times consuming. Before the staff member assumes his responsibilities, he and the senior pastor need to have a complete agreement about any school attendance, even on a part-time basis.

The staff member should know how much he can be away from his post to participate in ministry elsewhere (as a workshop leader or retreat speaker, for example) or to attend such things as seminars, conferences, or conventions—including general councils and other officially sponsored meetings. Policy should include whether the church will pay expenses. Such policy should take into consideration how the particular activity will increase the staff member's knowledge of his field and inspire his efforts in his ministry.

The hours a staff member is to work in the office is important. They should be specific: a time to report for work and a time to leave the office—unless on visitation or fulfillment of some other staff responsibility outside the office. The job of pastor or church staff member is not a 40-hour per week position. Forty hours a week just doesn't allow one to pastor a church with any degree of success. The pastor should never expect more of a staff member than he is willing to do himself, but he has a right to expect a staff member to give his very best.

First Assembly, Memphis, had a workday schedule in its operational manual that read:

> Full-time employees in the professional area will generally observe office hours from 9:00 A.M. until 5:00 P.M. each day, Monday through Saturday, for the accomplishment of their job assignments, with a one-hour lunch period and one day off during the week as assigned by the senior pastor. Staggered office hours may be observed by these employees with the knowledge and consent of the senior pastor. These employees will also be required to work additional hours in visitation, attending all church meetings, and any other assignment dealing with their specific area of responsibility.

Each member of the staff should be allowed at least one full day off, a day when he is never called upon to fulfill any task except in an extreme emergency. Many years ago we had a young man named

Forest Arnold on our staff. He had just finished college, was married, and the father of one child. On one of his days off I noticed that he was in his office. I went in and asked him what he was doing there on his day off. He replied that he just had some paperwork he had to get finished, whereupon I said to him very firmly, and I hope kindly, "You go home and spend this time off with Virginia and your baby, and don't you ever come to this office again on your day off unless it is an extreme emergency."

Many years later, when Mildred and I were having dinner with this couple, who by this time were grandparents, they told us the command I gave to him as a young youth pastor made them realize how important it was for them to have some time together. They believed this was the key to the beginning of their most happy and fruitful life together. Today, both are instructors at Central Bible College and are in demand nationwide for family enrichment seminars.

It is extremely important that pastors and staff members work energetically and faithfully at their jobs during working hours; it is equally important for their physical and mental welfare that they spend time with their families and in recreation of some type.

Before assuming a position on the staff, one should ask for a job description that would outline his responsibilities. Often a person is employed as an assistant pastor with no specific understanding of what his duties will be. The new staff member enters into his new job with eagerness and enthusiasm only to discover that he is too aggressive, and the pastor becomes unhappy with him for overstepping his authority. Or the opposite occurs: A person goes on a staff without getting a clear understanding of what is expected and in fear of displeasing the pastor he does very little. So he is branded as lazy and unconcerned about the church and its ministry.

A good job description would solve those problems. An incoming staff member would then know what he should and should not do, what is and is not expected of him. Then he can determine very easily whether he is doing his job. (See the sample job descriptions at the end of this chapter.)

Directing Staff Members

The pastor must have the oversight of the total church program because he must give an account to God and the church for the total operation.

For example, if a paid director of music is on the staff he should have a free hand in selecting music, musicians, and choir members. However, the total musical program should be within the guidelines established by the pastor and church. The pastor should feel free to make recommendations from time to time to the music director and expect them to be carried out. The same rule should apply to all departments and staff members.

To avoid confusion and assure good relationships and efficient service, a detailed job description should be provided for all staff members. They should, therefore, have a clear understanding of the responsibilities and the authority each position carries. The job description for each position will differ in each church according to the responsibilities assigned to a staff member. (Note again the examples at the end of this chapter.)

Limitations are placed on assistants by some pastors. For example, some pastors do not want their assistants to perform weddings and funerals. I believe that assistants should participate in all phases of the ministry of the church. In any case, these matters need to be clearly set forth at the beginning.

An assistant should possess qualities that go beyond the job description: Loyalty to God, the church, and the pastor is the number one prerequisite. Some shortcomings may be tolerated on the church pastoral staff, but not disloyalty. It should receive no second chance: One violation should automatically terminate a staff member.

Any time a staff member is in disagreement with the pastor or the church about its policy and action, he should be free to express his convictions to the pastor. If his differences cannot be satisfactorily reconciled, it then is best that he seek a place elsewhere to work for the Lord.

All members of the staff must respect the senior pastor. A pastor cannot demand respect; he must command it by his deportment, ability, leadership, communication, integrity, knowledge, and spiritual qualities. If a staff member cannot hold the pastor in the highest respect, it is best that the staff member's service be terminated. Mutual respect should be a prominent characteristic of the staff and the leadership of the church.

An absolute requirement for success on the staff of a church is a genuine spiritual concern for the people with whom one works. However otherwise qualified one may be, if the touch of God is not upon his life and ministry, he does not qualify as a good member of the staff. The staff members' spiritual concern will reflect itself in their dealing with the people person-to-person.

Any successful pastoral staff member must be aggressive. The church of Jesus Christ is not to just "hold the fort," but to break down the "gates of hell." A good staff member is not just to administer the already established policies of his department but to constantly seek ways to improve and advance the department.

A member of the church staff should never have to be told to do something that needs attention in his department. Within the framework of his responsibility he should take the initiative in developing plans and programs for his department.

A staff member must be prompt in keeping appointments, reporting to work, and starting meetings for which he is responsible. Staff members should follow through on any task assigned to them by the job description or by the pastor. The senior pastor does not have time to check and recheck to see if an assigned task is being attended to.

I used to say to my pastoral staff, numbering ten men and women: "I have a consuming passion to do as much for God as possible in the years alloted me or before our Lord returns, so when I request that one of you do something, it is important enough that I want it done immediately! None of you has been or will ever be treated like an 'errand boy' or 'flunkie,' but as equals in the work of God. So when you are asked to do a thing, I am not requesting that you do it at your convenience or that you give it a priority somewhere among the things that you are going to get around to. The very fact that it is assigned to you from the senior pastor means that it has priority already."

At no time does the staff member have the authority not to follow through on, or discontinue, any program or task that is assigned to him by the job description or by the senior pastor. When a program is not successful and the staff person in charge thinks he has an idea for improving it, or believes it should be discontinued, he should refer this to the senior pastor and the staff.

A staff member should possess, or develop, alertness. He should be alert to what is transpiring in the church program, the church service, the staff meetings, etc. One does not get ahead in the business or professional world by being dull, half-asleep, or uninterested in what is going on around him. A good staff member is alert to opportunities. Someone has said the difference between success and failure is the ability to know an opportunity when it comes your way and seize upon it.

A good attitude is very important for the staff member. A defeatist attitude means that he will go down to defeat. An attitude of enthusiasm means that he will inspire and encourage others to be enthusiastic. Both attitudes are contagious. The work of God is the work of faith. A defeatist attitude is to be defeated before you begin. One must inspire others to work with him and to assist him. One can do this only if he has the proper attitude toward the project.

The staff member must always be a team member. His primary responsibility is his department, but his secondary responsibility is the whole church and every member. He will never be successful as a staff member if he is concerned only with one department. As the whole church goes on to success, he will go on to success as a member of the team. The success of the church will be a team effort with the whole staff sharing in whatever success the church enjoys.

The senior pastor is able to minister to the people only as he comes to know them. The staff member must keep the senior pastor informed at all times about what is transpiring in his department and in the church. With a large congregation strong contact with every member of the church is impossible for the senior pastor. To know how members are progressing spiritually or to know about any problems that may be developing in their lives, the senior pastor needs the eyes and ears of his staff people. In this way he may better minister to the congregation.

The Staff Conference

Communicating with the staff is of the utmost importance to the successful church. Perhaps no other administrative tool is more important to good communication and successful operation of the church program than *regular* conferences with the staff.

Whether the pastor has only one assistant or a dozen, it is vital that he meet with them regularly at a specific time on a stated day, preferably each week. The staff conference will promote teamwork.

When working with a staff, impress upon them that the work of the staff is a team effort.

Such meetings should not be just a social chat over coffee, but a serious, well-planned conference of paid ministerial staff where reports are received, the progress of the church is evaluated, and plans are made and projected for implementation. Such conferences should be at regular times, have an agenda, and provide a free exchange of ideas and evaluations. Allow enough time for these weekly conferences to cover the total church ministry. Regular meetings with clerks, secretaries, custodians, and others employed by the church is also helpful.

The staff conference will assure good communication among staff members. Many problems are caused by our failure, or inability, to communicate. This is true of nations, families, individuals, and even churches.

Staff conferences make it possible to check carefully our communication. Do we understand our responsibilities? Are we carrying out our assignments?

The staff conference enables the pastor and his staff to evaluate, project, and implement plans for God's work. It is important that the pastor and his staff weekly evaluate the church work program and ministry. For example, what was the Sunday school attendance last Sunday? Was the attendance an increase or decrease? What contributed to the increase or decrease in attendance? The total church activities for the week can be evaluated, and by so doing, weaknesses and strengths can be pointed up, enabling the church to improve in every department.

The staff meeting will enable the staff to project plans for the future. For example, how to involve the church membership in an upcoming evangelistic campaign; how to involve the total church in earnest, sincere travailing prayer; how to ensure the best possible attendance; how to advertise these crusades; how to provide the best possible music; how to mobilize needed personal workers.

If each member of the staff goes his or her separate way without proper communication and without planning, programming, and sharing with his fellow laborers, he is subject to becoming individualistic and even noncooperative in the overall ministry of the church.

A prerequisite for leadership is the ability to communicate one's vision, faith, dreams, concerns, and desires, and to inspire and encourage staff people to assist in reaching those goals. A staff conference should provide a vehicle for the senior pastor to inspire and encourage his staff to assist in fulfilling the vision he has for God's work.

Staff conferences should provide a meeting of minds for those striving to fulfill the eternal purpose of the church. Although the conference should entertain the free exchange of opinions, ideas, and philosophies, by the time the staff conference is over, if possible, a consensus should be achieved. Of necessity, there must be one voice. And differences among staff members must never be paraded before the congregation.

The pastor is responsible to God and the congregation for all decisions having to do with the church and its ministry, so his opinions must prevail. On more than one occasion, however, my opinions have been changed when I heard the ideas presented by one or more members of my staff. So there is great value in not only expressing your own opinions, but hearing the opinions and ideas of others. The security of knowing that the pastor makes the final decision can open the way for free discussion. The most important gift a pastor can give staff members is to be secure enough to offer this freedom.

Some pastors arrange an annual retreat for the ministerial staff. Such a retreat usually is planned for 2-4 days and nights, at which time there is a very frank discussion of the weaknesses and strengths of the church. Every department and every facet of the ministry of the church is brought into focus. The various ministries of the church are analyzed and evaluated.

Plans for the coming year are projected and means of implementing such plans are outlined. The church calendar for the whole new year is discussed. Dates are written into the church calendar for various events during the year. This eliminates the problem of departments and groups planning events on the same dates.

These annual retreats are usually held in a resort area. On the front end, however, the pastor must decide if this is just to be a social get-away for his people or if they are going to devote some hard work and serious consideration to the church and its needs.

Of course, some time for recreation can be arranged. I would suggest, though, that most of the time be planned for prayer and serious discussion of the church and its ministry. A time of recreation for the staff and their families is good, but I prefer to have such times separated from the annual staff retreat. The primary task is to get on with fulfilling the eternal purpose.

Reporting and Accounting

Good administration is being able to delegate responsibilities and require an accounting for said assignments. Staff members should give an account of their activities weekly. (All of us are likely to do a better job on any task if we know we must give an account.)

Such reports, in detail, may be given in the weekly staff conference. In this way the senior pastor is able to get an overview of the church operation, alerting him to any need for special help.

In addition to the verbal report made by staff members of First Assembly, Memphis, which were recorded and became a permanent record, each staff member was required to turn in a weekly visitation report. The results of such visits were reported whether the visit was to a sick member, an absentee, a prospect, or a person needing pastoral care. A study of these weekly reports by the senior pastor provided him an important briefing on the people being ministered to and those needing special help.

Each staff member was required to turn in a monthly report. The report form was designed especially for a particular department, to enable an overview of the department for that month. (See the example of a report sheet on the following page.)

For example, the children's director reported each Sunday's attendance and the average for the month in the children's church, Missionettes, the children's division of Sunday school, the children's choir rehearsals, the nursery, and other children's activities, such as the "Kids Klub." The report form also provided space for special activities during the month and visitation of absentees, prospects, mothers with new babies, and so forth.

Because the senior pastor is responsible for the total church, he needs to know what is going on in every department of the church. More than just verbal reports, he needs facts and figures to study, comparing them with last month's and with last year's. Such reports become history that can be of great benefit from month to month

EDUCATION DEPARTMENT

MONTHLY REPORT

MONTH	YR

REGULAR ACTIVITIES

ACTIVITY		Week Ending Date:	Week Ending Date:	Week Ending Date:	Week Ending Date:	Week Ending Date:	Average or Total
SUNDAY SCHOOL	Adult Division						
	Youth Division						
	Children's Division						
	TOTAL						
BUS MINISTRY	SUNDAY AM — Bus 1						
	Bus 2						
	Maxi 1						
	Maxi 2						
	Sun. Night*						
	Wed. Night*						
WORKER TRAINING	S.S. WORKERS CONFERENCES — Adult						
	Youth						
	Children						
SPECIAL MINISTRIES							

Remarks: *co-ordinated activities

_____

Signed

and year to year in directing the church and its various ministries. You do not really know where you are going until you know where you have been!

The successful pastor is an administrator. He administrates the whole church. His responsibility is to know in detail the activities of all departments and to provide oversight and leadership, under God, for all the people, from the youngest to the oldest.

The mutual attitudes of the pastor and the staff contribute a great deal to the success or failure of the overall church program. If our attitude is one of love, respect, admiration, cooperation, consideration, and appreciation, we usually receive the same response. We reap what we sow.

The pastor should be very careful to give consideration to the desires, ambitions, positions, and feelings of staff members. The pastor must never think of the assistant as just an employee, nor should the assistant ever think of the senior pastor as just his "boss." They should practice understanding, love, respect, and admiration for each other.

At the time of my retirement as pastor of First Assembly, Memphis, the executive staff consisted of five ordained ministers, one minister with specialized credentials, and four laypeople. In public service and in print we referred to each clergyman as Pastor So-and-So. Our people thought of them as pastors. The congregation understood the chain of command, but they also respected the assistants as pastors, not just as employees of the church.

The pastor must be very careful to never embarrass his staff members before others, nor should the assistant ever under any circumstances take issue with the pastor in public or before others.

If the congregation appreciates the assistants, chances are they will think a great deal more of the senior pastor. On the other hand, the assistant should take advantage of all opportunities to express his appreciation for the pastor and his leadership.

The goal of both the pastors and staff should be to create a sense of belonging for all members of the staff—a team spirit. The pastoral staff ought to work as a team, sharing in the credit as well as any failure.

The following job descriptions are only examples. Each pastor and congregation should adapt job descriptions according to what their particular church requires. A job description in one church might differ for the same position in another church.

Associate Pastor
Job Description

Responsibilities:
Direct pastoral and administrative staff in absence of pastor
Direct evangelism and discipling programs
Direct overall visitation program
Visit and counsel with members who need special spiritual help
Counsel with those requesting such service
Direct distribution of books, periodicals, tracts, and other literature for purpose of evangelism
Assistant editor of church paper
Supervise news releases, brochures, and advertising
Supervise church photography and graphics room
Assistant radio and television director
Assist senior pastor in any other field of ministry where requested
Keep the senior pastor informed of all phases of the work assigned

Minister of Pastoral Care
Job Description

Responsibilities:
Visit those who make a decision for Christ
Visit first-time visitors to church who request a visit
Visit all new members immediately after they join the church
Visit church absentees
Visit Sunday school prospects and absentees in cooperation with director of education
Visit all hospitalized members and others who request a visit
Visit shut-ins confined to their homes, nursing homes, etc.
Direct prayer room ministry
Select and train personal and prayer room workers
Direct bus service for Wednesday and Sunday night services
Direct extension ministry in nursing homes, prisons, etc.

Perform any other visitation or other work directed by the senior pastor

Visit all families in which a death has occurred

Be responsible for all floral arrangements, food, transportation, family contact, etc., in case of a death

See that all hospitalized receive a get well card

Perform all other tasks assigned by pastor

Director of Education and Children's Division
Job Description

Responsibilities:

Direct overall Christian education program of the church

Coordinate Sunday school work of all departments

Direct all activities of the Sunday school

Supervise all Sunday school records

Direct all Sunday school visitation and follow-up

Promote Sunday school attendance

Direct all special Sunday school campaigns

Direct Sunday school workers training programs

Select all Sunday school personnel in cooperation with the senior pastor, staff, and department superintendents

Prepare budget for total Sunday school and supervise Sunday school budget expenditures

Be responsible for all Sunday school literature, materials, and equipment

Be an example for Sunday school staff in visitation of absentees and prospects

Oversee audio-visual equipment used in Sunday school

Work with adult pastor in educational program for adults

Work with youth pastor in educational program for all youth

Direct and develop Sunday school bus ministry

Direct spiritual life and training of all children

Supervise children's division in Sunday school

Direct children's church

Direct cradle roll department

Direct nursery and nursery workers

Direct Missionettes and other children's groups

Cooperate with director of recreation for children

Direct primary day camp and kids' camp

Be responsible for children's choirs (in cooperation with minister of music)

Visit mothers of newborn babies

Plan, promote, direct vacation Bible school

Prepare budget for children's division and supervise budget expenditures

Perform all other duties assigned by the senior pastor

Keep the senior pastor informed of all activities in the Sunday school and children's division

Minister of Music
Job Description

Responsibilities:

Direct all music for church services, radio, and television

General supervision of all choirs and other musical groups

Oversee maintenance of all musical instruments, such as pianos and organs

Direct music department budget expenditures

Care for TV and radio music, props, etc.

Oversee upkeep and utilization of all sound equipment

Prepare and edit radio tapes, tapes for sale, and missionary tapes

Perform all other duties assigned by the senior pastor

Keep the senior pastor informed of all phases of the work for which the music minister is responsible.

4

The Pastor and His Congregation

The calling of a pastor is of tremendous importance to the pastor and the church. The clumsy way some churches go about securing a pastor is alarming.

One of the weaknesses in the church/pastor relationship is the short tenure of the pastor. Roy C. Price writes, "Southern Baptists have found that a pastoral crisis occurs about every eighteen months of ministry. . . . [Southern Baptist Convention] pastors move on the average of every 18-20 months."[1] Many other denominations would have a similar record, if not worse. A pastor who stays no more than two years in a pastorate is really only the preacher and not the pastor in the full sense of the word.

At the time I retired, after thirty-seven years as pastor of the church in Memphis, every member of the church board had become a member of the church during my tenure. Only one of the twelve men on the board had ever had any experience in changing pastors, and that was in a smaller church in a distant state.

After my retirement, the church board appointed a search committee that proceeded immediately, but cautiously and prayerfully, to find a successor. After some weeks had gone by, a man who had become a member of the church several years before said to me, "Pastor, this church does not know anything about calling a pastor. Now take the church that I grew up in. We had a new pastor every two or three years. We never did anything else much, but we were experts in calling pastors." It is certainly true that churches that change pastors every two or three years don't do much more than provide pastoral experience for a number of men. They accomplish very little else for the cause of Christ.

The conscientious pastor should educate his congregation in calling a pastor. They should put together, very carefully and prayerfully, a procedure for securing a new minister. This is always a critical time for the congregation. It has been said, "What the pastor is, the church becomes." Therefore, the congregation should decide just what type of pastor would be best for leading them in fulfilling the purpose of the church.

The official board usually becomes the pulpit committee when the pulpit becomes vacant. A search committee, from members of the board or representative members from the overall membership, may be appointed.

The responsibility of the search committee is to consider all nominees, applications, and recommendations. Members of the church should have the privilege of submitting to the committee the name of any minister in good standing. After prayerful consideration of all names submitted, the search committee should make a smaller list of those to be seriously followed up.

The following information should be secured regarding the prospective candidates: Where they are now ministering; where they have pastored; the result of their ministry in other places; whether they really have a pastor's heart or are just looking for a place to preach; how long they have stayed in other churches; whether they are fitted with spirituality, character, personality, experience, training, attitude, and wisdom to pastor this particular church.

A pastor should not be selected solely on his ability to preach. Pastoring is more than just preaching! This points up the danger of inviting a minister to preach for a weekend and then voting on him as pastor. In so doing, the church may get an excellent preacher, but a very poor pastor. Most preachers have at least two or three good sermons!

Search committees should seek information from district officials regarding any person being considered as pastor. Some committees, after securing certain information and recommendations, have visited (without the prospective candidate's knowledge) the church where he is pastoring to observe how he preaches and leads his congregation in worship on an ordinary Sunday.

When the search committee has decided that a minister would be a viable choice for pastor, they should arrange an interview with him, perhaps following the service they visit. After the interview they should make a recommendation to the official board to invite the prospective pastor to the church for an interview with the board and to preach for a weekend. If the search committee and the board of deacons recommend the prospect to the congregation, a vote of the membership should be taken in keeping with the church constitution and bylaws. Under no circumstance should more than one person be voted upon in each election.

The procedure will take some time, but the church can buy itself some real problems by rushing into calling a pastor. An interim pastor could fill in for several weeks or months if necessary. Usually retired pastors, returned missionaries, local preachers, or assistant pastors are available. However, no person should be selected as interim pastor or preacher who might be a candidate for the pastorate. This could create some confusion.

The Pastor Must Love His People

To successfully pastor, a minister must be more than a good preacher and teacher. He must have more than administrative abilities, a well-educated mind, a charming personality, physical attractiveness. He must be a faithful shepherd to guide, protect, and feed the flock. He must love his people, be compassionate, be an example, build confidence, command respect, strive to communicate. He must lead the people into the things of God with power and authority. He must be able to say, "This is the way, walk ye in it."

The pastor's love must not be just for the congregation as a whole, but for each individual: those who respond favorably to him and those who do not, those who are faithful, cooperative, supportive, and those who are not.

Perhaps the simplest way to illustrate this love of the pastor for his congregation is the parents' love for their children. Parents love the lovely child, as well as the unlovely, rebellious child. Parents love the healthy, robust child, as well as the weak, sickly child.

Over the years, from time to time, I have heard pastors say, "Since so-and-so left the church, we are getting along fine. I am glad they are gone. There are a few more that I would like to lose." I have never been able to understand such statements.

In some fifty years as a pastor, I can truthfully say I never lost a member from the congregation that I wanted to see leave. Of course, I lost members from time to time, but if it was for some other reason than a move from the city I was inclined to feel that I had failed at some point. I think I felt the way parents must feel when a child grows up and rejects their counsel and love. Even though the child has become responsible for his own conduct, parents search their past to see if and how they may have failed. Pastors are not called of God to get rid of people, but to lead them to Christ and preserve them for eternity.

In most cases, individuals respond favorably to love. If we love them, they respond in kind. Of course, exceptions occur, but a good pastor continues to love those who may not love him.

Love is manifested not only in words, but in actions and attitudes. Some pastors are not in love with people, they are in love with the concept of love—just as the man who said, "I love humanity, but I do not like people." Whatever the pastor's ability, gifts, and commitments, Paul reminds us that even if we have such gifts as prophecy, knowledge, wisdom, and though we give our bodies to be burned and our goods to feed the poor, and though we have theology and outward philanthropy, unless love abides in us, we will not have the approval of God. Without love, it is impossible to please God. (See 1 Corinthians 13.)

The service that we render for our Lord and His church must be motivated by love. We cannot work successfully for the cause of Christ if we work mechanically, or by rote. We must work for God because we are motivated by love.

We must love before we can win souls. We must become emotionally involved to win souls. Soul winning is not a cold, calculated business. You cannot win souls with just programs, computers, and organizations. It is a spiritual work and the spiritual involves the whole of man—spirit, soul, and body.

The Early Church preachers experienced this love. It is expressed in the words of Peter and John to the authorities when they said, "We cannot but speak the things which we have seen and heard" (Acts 4:20). It was exemplified in the work and ministry of Paul and in his words when he said, "For the love of Christ constraineth us; because we thus judge, that if one died for all, then were all dead: and that he died for all, that they which live should not henceforth live unto themselves, but unto him which died for them" (2 Corinthians 5:14,15).

Unfortunately our word *love*, like the man who went down from

Jerusalem to Jericho, has fallen among thieves and been robbed of its meaning, stripped of its significance, and left dying by the wayside. The word *love* reveals both the beauty and the poverty of our English language. Whether it be the infatuation of an adolescent boy or girl under a summer moon or the fifth marriage of a four-time divorced Hollywood star or what a mother reveals when she risks her life to rescue her infant child from a burning building—we call it love. It may be an affair of illicit passion, a missionary abandoning the comforts of home for the salvation of aborigines in the African bush, or the Son of God on a Roman cross hanging stark against the darkened sky . . . no matter, we call it love.

In so-called Christian circles, love, of course, is everybody's word. Perhaps that is the trouble—it is just a word. A verbalism instead of a verity.

The word *love* in modern-day usage has been corrupted. But, thank God, the emotion of love, the act of love, the force and power of love, remain unchanged.

In Greek, the language of the New Testament, there are at least three words for love. The Greek word for love that the New Testament reserves for high and holy purposes is *agape*. When the New Testament speaks of God's love for man, it is *agape*. When it speaks of the Christian's love for God, it is *agape*, and much of the time the Christian's love for each other is *agape*.

There is a Greek word for passion and sexual feelings, *eros*; there is another Greek word for fraternal and family affection, *philos*. In the New Testament, these two are passed over in favor of a term that has a minimum of emotion and a maximum of conviction—*agape*.

God is love. If we are to represent our Lord in this world, we must manifest love for our fellowman.

Jesus said, "By this shall all men know that ye are my disciples, if ye have love one to another" (John 13:35). Love is the measuring rod that Jesus gave to His disciples. Love for one another was a mark of the genuine Christian in New Testament times. It is also evidence of genuine Christianity today.

The Cross is never redemptive until we have allowed it to correct us in the field of our human relationships. We are never in right relationship with God until we are right with our fellowman. The love of the Early Church was built upon the theological concept of the oneness of the body of Christ, that the whole body of Christ (which is the Church) functions as a single body.

Christ gave us the Parable of the Good Samaritan, reminding us that it is unthinkable for a priest or a pastor or even a Christian to ever "pass by on the other side" when there are wounds to be treated, hungers to be satisfied, and needs of men to be met. The New Testament church was a fellowship of people who cared.

In Revelation 2 the Ephesian church was doctrinally correct, outwardly sound, with stern discipline and a working program, but it was losing the very force that motivated its activities. It was losing its love. This loss of love possibly began with its pastors. It is possible to be orthodox and fundamental and, at the same time, be far from loving. One may be as straight as a gun barrel theologically and just as empty—void of that force that motivates one to do effective work for Christ.

Love is more than just an attitude, a concept, a theory, a gospel, an emotion. It is action. It is a verb: "God so loved the world that He gave."

The better a pastor knows his congregation, the more effective he should be in ministering to them. To be an effective pastor, he must be touched with the feeling of their infirmities. This is a strong argument for long pastorates. Until a pastor has lived with a congregation, shared their joys, victories, and triumphs, as well as their disappointments, sorrows, and defeats, he is little more to them than a preacher.

The Pastor Must Be Compassionate

Christ is our High Priest "touched with the feeling of our infirmities" (Hebrews 4:15). Just as the pastor is the "under shepherd," Christ being the Chief Shepherd, he is also the "under priest," touched with the feeling of the infirmities of his people.

However much ability, education, and personal charm we may have, we will never fulfill God's purpose and plan for us as ministers of the gospel without a passion for souls, a pity that yearns, a love unto death, a fire that burns.

We must be motivated by the same spirit that caused the Master to pause when He heard the cry of blind Bartimeus, encountered the sorrow of the widow of Nain, or looked upon the affliction of the man let down through the roof. We must feel some of the compassion He felt when He saw the needy, confused multitudes that were "as sheep having no shepherd." The Scriptures tell us that He was moved with compassion. This is a beautiful and powerful expression. "Moved with compassion"—it reveals a kind of sympathy that does not exhaust itself in sentiment but issues in action.

The true pastor must have some of the compassion Jesus felt when He, weeping, looked over Jerusalem and said, "Oh, Jerusalem, Jerusalem . . . how often I would have gathered thy children together . . . and ye would not" (Matthew 23:37).

Only shallow souls and shallow minds can look upon sinning humanity with unconcern, with a sort of complacent detachment. Men called to the ministry must be profoundly disturbed with the follies, the iniquities, and the stupidities of their fellow beings.

Preachers of the gospel must feel as Paul felt when he cried out, "Woe is me if I preach not the gospel." They must certainly experience the same motivation and driving force within their souls that caused the apostles to say to the authorities who threatened and told them not to preach anymore in the name of Christ, "We cannot but speak what we have seen and heard."

The Pastor Must Build Confidence

One cannot overemphasize how important it is that the congregation have confidence in the pastor. They must have confidence in his absolute integrity, his ability to lead, his sincerity of purpose, and his concern and interest in their welfare.

When the church and the board have utmost confidence in the pastor, he can do almost anything he desires to do, within reason, in carrying out the program and ministry that God has laid on his heart for that particular church.

To build this confidence, the pastor must be absolutely honest with his congregation, his board, and other officers. However nonessential he thinks the details, the pastor must never get himself out on a limb to where the people believe that he did not tell them all of the truth, that he was endeavoring to mislead them in some manner.

The pastor must strive to communicate. It is generally held that the majority of the problems of the world—internationally, nationally, domestically, and personally—are caused by man's inability to communicate with man.

Communication involves not only telling our ideas, and conveying our position, but also listening to others and understanding their position.

A pastor should try to communicate with all the congregation, every segment, whether he feels they will agree with him or not. He should not feel that a man is against him personally because he disagrees with his policy. Neither can he allow a member's personality traits to affect his pastoral relationship to that person.

A good leader is able to distinguish between policy and principle. One can compromise policy (the way of doing things) but he should never compromise principle.

An important part of good communication and proper relationship is to understand the responsibilities and authority in the various areas to which we have been assigned.

So often trouble develops at this point because leaders, board members, and others do not know the authority, limits, and responsibilities inherent in the positions assigned to them. In cases of this kind, individuals or boards often assume authority that does not rightfully belong to them.

A good, clear church constitution and bylaws approved by the church and respected by all will do much to produce harmonious relationships in this area. The larger churches especially should have an operational manual dealing with employee operations, employee benefits, job descriptions, use of church properties, financial policies and procedures, and general information about various departments and ministries of the church.

The reason the congregation does not always go along with the pastor on some projects and programs is that they do not understand them. The pastor has failed to communicate these projects to his people. A pastor cannot expect the people on the spur of the moment to decide to do a thing that he has been considering, and praying about, for months.

The Pastor Must Command Respect

You cannot demand respect, you must command it—by your

deportment, your ability, your leadership, your communication, your integrity, your knowledge, and your spiritual qualities.

A building block of respect is trust: You do not respect the person you do not trust. And you do not trust the person you do not know.

When Roy Price was new as the senior pastor at First Alliance Church in Louisville, Kentucky, he was frustrated by the low level of trust the congregation had for him.

When he expressed this to a lady in his church, she asked him, "Do you really expect people to automatically trust you because you were called here?"

He replied, "I thought that came with the job."

Whereupon she said, "Some of us have been burned and we need time to get to know you."

What causes getting "burned," and the development of mistrust? According to Price, "Dishonesty heads the list . . . from withholding information to manipulative techniques. For example, one pastor claimed a vision from God to validate a fund-raising idea. His laymen had difficulty refuting the plan . . . how could they fight God? It did not take long for them to realize they had been manipulated and trust was undermined."

This is one of Mr. Price's conclusions about how trust is developed: "It parallels man's relationship with God." We trust God because He's proven himself to be as good as His Word.[2]

When a pastor's behavior is above reproach, when he communicates well—when he's as good as his word—he will have respect.

The Pastor Must Provide Strong Leadership

The successful pastor must lead with authority. To exercise authority and leadership does not mean to dictate, to be a tyrant. It means rather to lead and guide in one's work with individuals, committees, boards, as well as the congregation. The pastor should be able to say, "This is the way, walk ye in it."

For more than fifty years I have served on district boards; for more than forty years, on the General Presbytery (the legislative body of the Assemblies of God) and for ten years, on the Executive Presbytery. In those many years on these important church boards, I have dealt with many church problems.

I have reached two definite conclusions out of those years of experience: One is that the great majority of the people in our churches love the Lord and want to do right in regard to the church program. Most of them have hearts that are right.

The second conclusion is that the great majority of serious church problems occur because of the lack of good leadership (leadership that is more often weak than bad). Poor leadership can create a situation that breeds misunderstanding, mistrust, and division— even for a later leadership.

If a pastor is to command respect, he must conscientiously evaluate and then have the ability and the courage to make proper choices. He cannot vacillate.

Working with a church board, for example, is tremendously important in the ministry. Many a pastor has failed because he did not know just how to work with the church board and other committees.

Before he assumes the pastorate a pastor should have a thorough understanding with the church and the board about his responsibilities, authority, and limits. A church constitution and bylaws should set forth these matters. I personally believe that it is wise for the pastor to serve as chairman of the board of deacons, elders, and trustees.

Many church boards assume authority and power that the church never intended them to have. In many cases, the board is not altogether to blame for this situation. For example, some churches change pastors every year or so. When the pastor resigns, the board usually has the responsibility of looking after the church until a new pastor arrives. In most cases, the board must take the initiative in securing a new pastor. When the new man arrives, he needs help and advice in getting oriented. The board provides that assistance. About the time he learns the ropes, he decides to move on to another church. So the board again must care for the church—meaning that the board is compelled to run the church most of the time.

A pastor must never permit personalities to affect his relationship with the members of his board or his congregation. He should never feel that a man is against him personally because he disagrees with the policies. The pastor must understand that there is a difference between policy (a course or plan of action, especially of administrative action) and principle (that which is inherent in anything, determining its nature or essence). A pastor can never be a successful leader if he cannot separate his position with regard to policy and principle.

If board members are not free to express their opinions and vote their convictions, they won't be able to contribute anything of worth to the church board. In my years as a pastor, I have found the church board to be a very important factor in the advancement of the cause of Christ. I always said to new board members: "We want you to feel perfectly free to express your opinions and vote your convictions on any matter that comes before this board. I also want you to understand that you do not work for me, and I do not work for you. We both work for our Lord and our church. Let us work together to fulfill the eternal purpose of the church of Jesus Christ."

It is impossible to overemphasize how valuable good deacons are when there is love, respect, and trust between them and the pastor. Many years ago I was about to employ a youth minister. I mentioned this young man to the board, as I often did before taking someone on staff. No one reacted to the announcement, one way or the other.

However, three or four days later, three members of the board asked me to have coffee with them. They told me that new information about the prospective youth pastor had come to them. They said, "Pastor, we think it would be a grave mistake to take this man on your staff, but that is your prerogative. If you do appoint him, we will stand by your decision and will stand with you whatever happens."

I had made a commitment and felt I had to proceed, but as time proved, it was a big mistake. The beautiful part of this story is that not one time in the many years after that occasion did any of these men, though they continued to serve on the board, remind me in any way that I had erred as a pastor. They were indeed real friends. Two of these godly men have since gone to be with the Lord; the third continues on the board. I shall ever be grateful to God for the privilege of working with such men.

The pastor should preside in board meetings with authority. In order to do that, he must be sure that he has all the facts and figures in hand and that he knows exactly what he is talking about. He must do his homework, gaining the confidence of the men to the degree that they know that whatever he tells them is correct and whatever mistakes he makes are genuine, not attempts to mislead them.

It is never wise to turn on the pressure of your influence and position to get your way in small matters. Save it for more important matters. It isn't wise to have favorites on the board or to discuss matters with certain board members privately before the matter comes before the whole board. This can lead to misunderstandings and mistrust, board members believing the pastor is playing politics and railroading certain projects through the board.

The authority of the pastor should not be one of office only. He should not be like the millionaire who said to one man, "I'll have you know, I am worth a million dollars"—only to have the man reply, "And not a penny more." The pastor should not have to remind people that since he holds that position, he has certain authority.

A minister exercises authority by his ability to command confidence and respect, to communicate his knowledge and wisdom, his integrity and his spiritual qualities.

For several years my family and I lived next door to the church in Memphis. Then it became necessary to tear the house down in order to erect the high school building. One day the director of the children's division drove into the church driveway with her small son, Chris, who was about six or seven years old. Seeing the moving van at our house, she said to Chris, "Did you know Pastor Hamill is moving?" After a moment of silence, Chris replied, "Mommy, do you mean Pastor Hamill isn't going to be the king of our church anymore?" Not one time had I ever mentioned my authority as pastor of that church. Yet no one had to tell this child or the congregation who was in charge. A successful pastor does not endeavor to force, pressure, or drive a congregation, a board, or a committee to do what he wants; he tries to show them, guide them, and lead them in doing the things he feels will advance the cause of Christ.

Strong leadership does not necessarily mean that the pastor will have his way in every detail of the operation of the church program. Strong leadership means that he will have his way in the important matters.

The Pastor Should Be an Example

The apostle Paul wrote to the young minister Timothy, "Be thou an example of the believers" (1 Timothy 4:12).

The most precious possession that any minister has is his character. What can we really accomplish for God without character? How much good can we do with a bad reputation? What value in the ministry is a good education if we do not have a good reputation? What good is a lot of talent if we do not have the confidence of the people to whom we endeavor to minister?

Let us strive for education, let us strive to develop our talent, let us work to enlarge our sphere of operation, let us plan to increase the effectiveness of our ministry, but first let us strive to be what God wants us to be. What we are is more important than what we know or who we know, or what we have done, what we do, or what we plan to do.

Although character may be what we are, what we are is reflected in what we do. Our behavior as representatives of God, as ambassadors for Christ, is so important we are admonished to walk circumspectly before all men and told that we are "epistle[s], . . . known and read of all men" (1 Corinthians 3:2). Dr. Richard C. Halverson has said, "The disciples learned from what Jesus did as well as what He said. His attitude under pressure and His response to those who came to Him were constant demonstrations of how to care for those in need."[3]

The pastor's attitude and conduct will usually be reflected in his congregation. If the pastor's attitude is one of faithfulness toward God, most of the congregation will reflect that attitude. If the pastor wants his congregation to be enthusiastic, then he must be enthusiastic.

If the pastor's attitude is one of defeatism, if he allows circumstances and conditions in the church or city or his life to defeat him or to cause him to take a defeatist attitude in his preaching or ministry, the congregation will become defeated.

The pastor who takes an attitude of indifference toward God and the church can hope for nothing else on the part of his congregation except indifference. The pastor who is indifferent concerning the work of God cannot hope to build anything except a small indifferent congregation.

Many clergymen's undoing has been their criticism of others. The attitude of being critical reflects itself in the pastor's congregation. The pastor should strive at all times to build confidence in the ministry, and teach his people to hold clergymen in the highest esteem. He should never criticize ministers to laymen. He should never criticize one member of the church to another. He should never gossip. These things are so important if the pastor is to build into his people the right attitude toward God and God's people.

Cooperation is an important attitude that the pastor must have. If he expects his congregation to have an attitude of cooperation toward him, then he must show a spirit of cooperation toward others: his organization, his church, his denomination, his fellow ministers. Cooperation is a two-way street.

If the pastor is noncooperative with others, his members often become noncooperative with him. If his attitude is one of criticism of his superiors, he will likely be the victim of criticism by his people. A critical spirit breeds distrust and disloyalty.

What the pastor is, the church has a way of becoming.

The Pastor Is the Shepherd

The apostle Peter, writing to ministers, said, "Feed the flock of God which is among you" (1 Peter 5:2). The New International Version translates this verse, "Be shepherds of God's flock that is under your care."

One of the responsibilities of the shepherd is to guide his sheep, to lead them. The Psalmist said that the Great Shepherd "leadeth me beside the still waters." Pastors who learn to lead the sheep are a great deal more successful than those who attempt to drive them.

The shepherd is to see that his flock is well-fed. The apostle Paul, giving final instructions to the ministers at Ephesus, said, "Take heed therefore unto yourselves, and to all the flock, over the which the Holy Ghost hath made you overseers, to feed the church of God" (Acts 20:28).

When Jesus asked Peter three times if he loved Him and Peter replied each time that he did, Jesus said, "Feed my sheep." No wonder Peter later wrote, "Feed the flock of God which is among you, taking the oversight thereof" (1 Peter 5:2).

The prophet Jeremiah gives us an idea of what the congregation is fed with and what a shepherd is supposed to instill: "I [the Lord] will give you pastors according to mine heart which shall feed you with knowledge and understanding." Again, God said to Jeremiah, "I will set up shepherds over them [the remnant Israel] which shall feed them: and they shall fear no more, nor be dismayed, neither shall they be lacking, saith the Lord" (Jeremiah 23:4).

In these days when life seems so complex and there is much distress, frustration, fear, and doubt, and an almost complete breakdown in our moral standards, a great need exists for wise counsel from the pastor. Counseling has become one of the great time consumers for the pastor, yet it is vital. To be able to share the love of God with those you try to help is the key to success in pastoral counseling.

The shepherd is to lead and guide his sheep beside the still waters and to the green grass, away from the dangerous precipice, the wild animals, and anything else that might harm them.

The apostle Paul was greatly concerned that the sheep be guided, counseled, nourished, and that they also be protected. He expressed this in his farewell address to the pastors at Ephesus when he said, "Take heed therefore unto yourselves, and to all the flock, over which the Holy Ghost hath made you overseers. For I know this, that after my departing shall grievous wolves enter in among you, not sparing the flock. Also of your own selves shall men arise, speaking perverse things, to draw away disciples after them" (Acts 20:28-30).

It becomes the responsibility of the pastor to guard the sheep against the wolves and those that would lead them astray. A pastor should never expose his people to false prophets and false doctrines. Pastors are sometimes tempted to invite a guest speaker, even though his character is questionable, simply because he is able to command a large crowd. But this is exceedingly dangerous, and a pastor of integrity with concern for his own people will not expose them to such a person.

Dr. Ramsey Pollard was president of the Southern Baptist Convention for two terms and pastor of the Bellevue Baptist Church in Memphis for twelve years. At his funeral the Reverend Elmer Bailey, his associate pastor in two pastorates for a total of twenty-five years, gave an appropriate paraphrase of 1 Corinthians 13 that may apply to the wise, understanding, loving pastor.

"Though I preach with the skill of the finest preacher, and have not understanding, I am become only a clever speaker, a charming entertainer, and though I have much training, so that I feel quite confident and have no understanding of the way my people think, it is not enough. And if I spend many hours on sermon preparation, and become tense and nervous with a strain, but have no understanding of the personal problems of my people, it is still not enough. The understanding preacher is very patient, very kind, is not shocked when his people bring their confidences, does not gossip, is not discouraged, does not behave in ways that are unworthy, but is at all times a living example to his congregation of the 'good way of life' of which he speaks. Understanding never fails, but whether there be materials, they shall become obsolete; whether there shall be methods, they shall become abandoned; for we know only a little and can pass on to our people only a little, but when we have understanding then all our efforts will become creative and our influence will live forever in the lives of our people. When I was a child I spoke with immaturity. My emotions were uncontrolled, and I behaved childishly. But now that I am an adult, I must face life as it is . . . with courage and with understanding. And now abideth skill, devotion, understanding; these three, but the greatest of these is understanding."

NOTES

[1]Roy C. Price, "Building Trust Between Pastor and Congregation," *Leadership* 1 (Spring 1980):50.

[2]Ibid., p. 48.

[3]Richard C. Halverson, "The Pastor and the Board: Maintaining a Healthy Relationship," *Leadership* 1 (Winter 1980):134.

5

The Pastor and His Community

A proper relationship to the community in which he lives and works is of utmost importance to the pastor. To succeed as a pastor he must have an interest in the community where he ministers, including the spiritual welfare of all the people and their economic, political, and physical welfare. James Bridges says, "A spirit of sectarianism circumscribes greatly the ministry and influence of a pastor in his community."[1]

Produce Confidence

In the community, the minister must produce confidence both in himself and his church. Influence is a most valuable asset to the ministry. How sad the minister whose personal life has been so lived that both private and public influence have been lost. When this occurs, his ministry will be ineffective and the work of the church in the community greatly impeded. The apostle Paul warns Titus, "Let no man despise thee" (Titus 2:15). *The Amplified Bible* renders this passage, "Let no one despise or disregard or think little of you—conduct yourself and your teaching so as to command respect." *The Living Bible* adds, "Don't let anyone think that what you say is not important."

We produce this confidence by a good attitude, proper conduct, and absolute integrity.

Our attitude must be one of sincerity, concern, love, honesty, and humility, coupled with firmness and stability. Our conduct in public and private affects our relationship to our community and determines to a great degree our influence.

E. S. Caldwell says, "The first essential in reaching any community involves public confidence. No one will come and accept the message preached by a church unless he is convinced the church actually lives up to what it claims to be. That means people must have some idea of what the church claims. Does it believe people burdened by guilt can be forgiven? Does it believe homes wrecked by sin can be restored? Does it believe sickness can be miraculously healed? Does it believe ineffective people can be changed into dynamic witnesses through a baptism of divine power? Such claims will attract attention providing people know about them. Then comes the acid test: Can the church deliver what it claims? If the answer is a resounding yes, then the church is on the way to winning public confidence. But if the church claims more than it can deliver, it writes its own epitaph."[2]

At Christmastime one year my wife and I had an occasion to change planes in Atlanta. The airport was crowded and the planes were filled with people. The chair assigned to me had a broken back. When the stewardess came along, I asked her, "Do you think there might be a vacant chair on this flight? If so, I would like to be reassigned. This chair is broken."

She replied, "Not likely, but there might be one or two."

"If there should be a vacant chair, will you please let me have it?"

She said she would and started walking away. When I said, "Don't forget me now," she whirled and snapped at me, "I told you that I would assign you any vacant chair."

I (perhaps not in a tone with which a clergyman should address a person) said, "Now, honey, don't get excited. I only want another chair if it's available."

Just at that moment a lady leaned across the aisle and said to me, "Aren't you Pastor Hamill? I see you on television every Sunday morning." I thought my wife was going to fall out of her chair laughing, but the incident gave me some food for thought about really being "epistles read and known."

I always enjoy the story that the superintendent of the Tennessee district, Gene Jackson, tells on himself. He had a morning in his office when everything seemed to go wrong. It was raining, sleeting, and snowing a little when he dropped in a short-order restaurant at noon and sat down at the counter to have a sandwich. A man sitting next to him turned and greeted him with "Good morning, how are you on this good and beautiful day!"

Jackson answered, "Well, it's not so beautiful to me, and I'm not doing too well today."

The man said, "You know, that's just the way I felt many days before I found the Lord Jesus Christ as my Saviour, and now every day is a beautiful day." The stranger proceeded to tell Jackson how the Lord had come into his heart and changed his life-style, his attitude, and made life really beautiful to him.

By this time the preacher had finished his sandwich and was about to leave when the new Christian said, "By the way, what kind of work do you do?"

Gene Jackson said to the stranger, "It's none of your business what I do," and walked out.

We never know when we may be called upon to identify ourselves, therefore our conversation, our attitude, our conduct, should be such that proudly we can say, "I am a preacher of the gospel."

The pastor must also maintain intellectual integrity with his community, to say nothing of his congregation. He should never make unfounded and questionable statements in public or in private. He should never take a position on an issue unless he is thoroughly convinced that it is the true and correct one.

The pastor should guard against a "credibility gap." His integrity should be such that if he takes a position or makes a statement with which the community disagrees, the people will respect him nevertheless. They know he sincerely believes he is doing and saying the proper thing.

In Memphis we once had a Jewish mayor. He invited me to have lunch with him. Upon my return to my office it occurred to me that in our conversation about economics, politics, and many other matters I had not witnessed to him about Jesus Christ. I felt condemned and asked the Lord to forgive me, promising that if I had such an opportunity again I would tell the mayor about Christ.

Some weeks later he again invited me to lunch. This time I talked to him about Jesus. He first told me his wife was a member of a Protestant church and that she took their two boys to church. I asked about his personal relationship to Jesus Christ. He replied that he could not accept Jesus as the Messiah, and that he was not prepared to believe in Him as Saviour. That day I went back to my office feeling I had failed, but with some degree of satisfaction that I had witnessed.

A few days later the mayor telephoned me. He said, "Jim, I need your help. I had to fire an employee of the city who drank on the job. He became absolutely irresponsible and we had to let him go." The mayor told me that he got to thinking about the man and that morning he had gone by to see how his family fared. He said he had seen to it that the family would make it all right financially during this difficult time, then he added, "But, Jim, this man needs something I can't give him. I believe he needs what you were talking to me about at lunch the other day. Would you go by and see him?"

I knew then that my witness had hit the target, and that even this Jewish mayor had confidence in my Lord's power to do something for this alcoholic and his family.

Integrity must mark the financial dealings of the pastor. He must be very careful about paying his financial obligations on time. This policy should also apply to the church that he leads. So often churches and pastors seem to get the idea that because they are a church or because they are clergymen they should not be expected to be prompt in paying their bills. This is not true.

This integrity should apply to such simple matters as promptly keeping appointments, or doing exactly what we promise when we promised. Pastors should guard well their word. When I was a child, I used to hear adults say, "His word is as good as his bond"—that his word was as good as a legal contract. That should be true of every pastor.

It is essential that the community have confidence in the pastor if he is to be in a position to be of help to his own congregation. Many years ago a young boy, a member of a family that belonged to First Assembly, was convicted along with some other teenagers of stealing an automobile. He had been sentenced to eight years in the penitentiary. The defense attorney moved for probation for him and subpoenaed me as a character witness. When I came to the witness stand, the judge simply said to the clerk, "Dispense with the swearing in of the pastor as a witness. I just want to talk to him." He asked me what I thought he ought to do with this eighteen-year-old boy about to be sent to the penitentiary for eight years. I told him that I was not very well acquainted with the young man, that I had only seen him at church a few times, but I did know his parents to be honorable, God-fearing Christians. I further stated that I believed that if this young man's sentence was probated and he came under the influence of the church, his life could be transformed. The church certainly would do more to rehabilitate him than eight years in an institution with hardened criminals.

The judge turned to this young man and said, "I'm going to probate you to the pastor. If I ever hear of your being willfully absent from Sunday school and church, I'm going to send you to the penitentiary for eight years."

(I was tempted to say, "Your Honor, will you please pass that sentence on all my congregation?")

That's not the end of that story. That young man did attend Sunday school and church. He later gave his heart and life to Jesus Christ, was married to a lovely girl, and though that has been many years ago, they still are regular worshipers and enthusiastic workers in the church. The confidence that the court had in the pastor and the church made possible this transformation.

Confidence in the pastor and the church is vital to the ministry and growth of the church. In 1972, when our church began a day school, one of the members of the board of trustees was a professor at Memphis State University. One day two other professors said to him, "We want to enroll our children in your new school."

E. W. Danley, the board member, asked, "Why do you want to do that? You don't know what the school will be like, what the standards will be, what level of education and discipline will be attained."

They expressed the highest confidence possible when they replied, "We know the school will be first class. We know the pastor and the church, and we know anything they promote will be all they claim it is."

Public Relations

Public relations covers a wide area of operation. However, I am referring to the pastor's communication, poise, and influence in the community where he lives and works. Public relations is keeping the community aware of the church and its activities, goals, and achievements. If a church wishes not to be ignored by its community, it must have good public relations.

E. S. Caldwell writes, "A church's public relations can be defined as the degree of understanding and goodwill it has achieved. It is a combination of publicity; promotion; and, most important of all, continued activities and relationships that enhance the church's reputation and ability to serve."[3]

The pastor himself can get better acquainted by becoming a part of a civic or service club in his community, such as Rotary or Kiwanis. Membership in such clubs will give him an entree into a circle of business and professional men that he probably would not otherwise have. It provides him an opportunity to serve his fellowman through the club's educational and charitable projects and to broaden the scope of his influence in the community.

In a small town where I pastored, men from my church were the presidents of all three civic and service clubs in that town, Rotary, Kiwanis, and the Chamber of Commerce. Through these men our church had influence for good in that little city.

In two of my former pastorates, I had daily radio programs. The church I had pastored the longest was the largest church of any denomination in a small town of some 10,000. I was well-known in every town I had pastored.

Memphis was another story. Coming to the largest city I had ever lived in and being unable to buy radio time or newspaper advertising, getting my church before the public was most frustrating. Eventually, through radio, television, newspapers, and other means of publicity and various efforts at good public relations, First Assembly became well-known throughout the Midsouth.

Once when I was scheduled to speak at the National Association of Evangelicals Convention in Washington, I noticed with great amusement that the *National Religious Broadcasters* magazine said that I was just about as well-known to Memphis as its famous son, Elvis Presley.

When *Decision* magazine, published by the Billy Graham Evangelistic Association, wrote the story about the Memphis church (calling it one of the great churches of America), they interviewed me, members of my staff, and members of the church. But they also interviewed neighbors; newspaper people; religious, political, and business leaders.

One of the quotes used in the article, and also recorded in the book *Great Churches of Today*, reminded me of those days when I struggled and wondered if I would ever be known in this city. The quote was from a Baptist pastor who said that when Dr. Robert G. Lee resigned as pastor of the great Bellevue Baptist Church in

Memphis, the spiritual mantle of leadership seemed to fall upon James E. Hamill. While I do not agree with this statement, it illustrated the fact that God had made it possible for me to lead my church into a place of prominence in the religious community.

A pastor can do numerous things to promote good public relations, such as joining in projects and programs that improve the community and the welfare of the people.

For many years First Assembly sponsored (at the church) a "City-County Employees Honor Day." All the city-county employees, as well as all elected officials, were invited to this special service. The pastor would commend the employees for various accomplishments, such as making our city one of the most beautiful, the fire department for being effective, the police department for protecting our lives and property, and so on. Then I would preach on a subject like "Righteousness Exalteth a Nation, But Sin Is a Reproach to Any People."

We had hundreds, and over the years thousands, of community employees attend. The mayor, city councilmen, county commissioners, judges, and other elected officials seldom were absent. This service brought many visitors to our church and some of them became members. It was an excellent opportunity to improve public relations, and it made our church well-known among city officials and employees.

With respect to this, I cannot overemphasize the importance of attitude. One's attitude toward his community and his church plays a tremendous role in the image his church projects in that community.

The church's attitude toward the community must not be one of antagonism or one of isolationism. If we are to fulfill God's purpose we must look upon the community and the world with love and concern and genuine interest. Everything that everybody else does is not bad. A holier-than-thou-attitude is the worst possible attitude to adopt toward one's community.

To project a good image the pastor must not be apologetic or ashamed of the church, its doctrine, its people. We do not need to always be on the defensive, but rather take the offensive.

An enthusiastic pastor and congregation certainly project a good image for the church. Enthusiasm is contagious. If you are sold on your church, other people will be too.

Participate in Worthwhile Projects

The pastor must not pull himself into a shell or isolate himself from the activities of his community and city if he expects community acceptance of his ministry. He should participate in civic and service programs for the betterment of his community so long as such programs do not affect his spiritual life or his influence for God. His work is a spiritual work, but a by-product of the spiritual is to be concerned about the welfare of others—physically, mentally, financially, and even politically.

Ministers should be a force for good in any community. The pastor whose integrity is unquestioned and who speaks up for righteous causes is usually highly respected and has the confidence of the community.

In late 1981 the Gallup Poll rated twenty-four professions and occupations based on "honesty and ethical standards." Among doctors, dentists, druggists, engineers, college teachers, bankers, lawyers, politicians, and others, the clergy had higher ratings.

Participation in Community Politics

The very purpose for establishing America was that men might find a land in which they could worship God according to the dictates of their own conscience.

Our forefathers laid a sure and solid foundation for a great nation. The cornerstone for that foundation was faith in God. Other foundation stones included reverence for God, respect for law, regard for freedom, and responsibility for personal character.

The three great forces in the lives of our forefathers were the home, the church, and the school. All developed upon faith in God.

In the school, the Bible was read and prayer was made. In fact, the Bible was a part of the curriculum. Even the highest institutions of learning were begun as church schools, including Harvard, Princeton, and Yale.

We have drifted a long way from our forefathers' concept of a godly nation. We have gone a long way from the principles on which this strong and free nation was built. The institutional church and its clergymen must share much of the blame for permitting our country to drift so far from the godly concepts of the founding fathers.

By no stretch of the imagination could any of us honestly believe that the framers of the Constitution intended to prohibit prayer and Bible reading in the public schools of this country. I firmly believe that Satan has a design to destroy our schools, our churches, and our homes, thus destroying our country.

I don't think anybody can successfully argue that the homes in America are not in trouble, or that public education is not in jeopardy, or that the institutional church has not lost its influence, power, and effectiveness.

There is absolutely nothing that should cause more concern in these days than the breaking up of marriages and homes. This is an alarming situation, and if we do not get some help from God in this area, the American home is absolutely, irrevocably gone.

The clergy and the mainline churches have failed to take a firm stand on those vital issues that preserve a strong, godly nation.

Annually, in April or May, *U.S. News and World Report* publishes a survey asking Americans to assess the influence that some 30 U.S. institutions and organizations have on decisions affecting the nation as a whole and determining the life-style of the people. In 1981 organized religion ranked 18. In 1982 the church had fallen to 25, and in 1983 the church ranked 26 out of 30 institutions and organizations that affect the decisions of the nation.

Among those that ranked well above the church were the White House, television, lobby and pressure groups, newspapers, labor unions, radio, and magazines.

In the list of institutions and organizations influencing the lifestyle of Americans, the family ranked 17 and the educational institutions 20. With the respect that Americans have for the integrity, trustworthiness, and ethics of the clergy, it would appear that the minister has been remiss in his responsibilities to use that influence for righteousness in his community and nation. God's Word declares, "Righteousness exalteth a nation: but sin is a reproach to any people" (Proverbs 14:34).

Great, strong, and free nations are not built upon ideologies, philosophies of government, political platforms, natural resources, military might, or the genius of its people. Nations are built upon the character of those charged with the responsibility of implementing those ideologies and philosophies, fulfilling those platforms and using natural resources and military might for the welfare, protection, and good of all the people in the country.

If our country is to return to those principles upon which this nation has been built—respect for law, regard for freedom, reverence for God, and responsibility for personal character—we must as individuals and as a nation return to God. The pastor, in his community, must assume a role of leadership in bringing the people back to God and to His Word. "When the righteous are in authority, the people rejoice: but when the wicked beareth rule, the people mourn" (Proverbs 29:2).

It has been said, "The only thing necessary for the triumph of evil is for good men to do nothing." The pastor who leads his congregation in a firm stand on moral issues will do much to make the community a decent place to live.

Nolan Harmon advises, "No minister should in public speech or sermon take part in partisan politics. The minister not only has the right, but is obligated to speak upon . . . moral questions in the pulpit or out of it, be the political . . . implications what they may. When a minister speaks . . . on burning moral questions . . . he must understand thoroughly every phase of the situation."[4]

The pastor's interest in politics and government should be confined, for the most part, to issues, not personalities. Back in the early days (1948) of my pastorate in Memphis, the famous political boss Ed Crump controlled politics in Tennessee, Memphis included. Few people dared oppose him on any issue. One day I read in the afternoon newspaper that that night a meeting of citizens interested in good government was to be held in one of the downtown hotels. More out of curiosity than for any other reason, I drifted into the meeting. The person scheduled to give the invocation did not show up. Someone recognized me and I was asked to give the invocation.

The first order of business was organizing a group called the Good Government League to interview, investigate, and endorse candidates for various offices in the city, county, and state. This was the group that later helped break the "Crumpmachine's" political grip in Tennessee. When, in this initial meeting, the directors were being nominated, to my amusement, a man stood and said, "I like the prayer that preacher prayed. I nominate him as a member of the board of directors." I stayed only a few minutes longer and left before the votes were counted. The next day I picked up the newspaper and to my chagrin the headline on page 1 of section 2 was a quote from my prayer. In the story, I was shocked to learn that I had been elected to the board of directors and was to chair a committee to interview candidates. I fulfilled my responsibility in this capacity, but soon learned that the pastor is not always comfortable in this environment.

From that time, I confined my interest to issues rather than personalities, which I believe is more in keeping with a pastor's responsibility.

Christians have political obligations. If the pastor fails, or is reluctant to lead his church into taking a firm stand on matters that affect the morals and well-being of the citizens of his community, he is remiss.

R. D. E. Smith, executive presbyter of the Assemblies of God, writes, "Whether or not that reluctance can be held responsible for the moral deterioration of our society, or whether the inactivity of the church is due to [a] principle of indifferentism, the fact remains that the moral and spiritual level of our society has suffered drastically within our lifetimes.

"Civic corruption and the exploitation of all forms of evil may be said to have been with us always, but the organized and openly avowed intent to destroy Christianity is of recent origin. The relative values of a permissive society produced and fostered by secular humanism are being written into the whole body of law. History is being distorted to accommodate a pluralistic society outside the Christian ethic.

"It has been well said that a problem, well stated, is half-solved. Therefore, the pastor's highest priority is to educate his people in these high principles by which the Christian lives."[5]

Ministerial Association

Most cities and towns have a ministerial association. The ministerial association creates a setting in which a group of ministers may work cooperatively to advance the cause of Christ. For the most part the ministerial association enjoys a respected place of influence in the community. Meade writes in *Reaching Beyond Your Pulpit*, "The minister who is too busy to associate himself with his brethren in the ministerial association or to attend conferences and conventions is circumventing his influence."[6]

The strength of the ministerial association varies from city to city.

The level of success and effectiveness of the association depends on the caliber and quality of the ministers who participate. The association can be a strong force in standing against evil in the community, or it can fall into the control of either those who are afraid to deal with any public issue or, worse, those who take a stand against almost all conservative issues.

For many years I was very active in the ministers' association in my city, serving on various committees and as vice-president and later as president. I believe the association in those years had a good influence on the morals and policies of our city. In recent years the ministers' association has come into the control of extreme liberals, making it impossible for conservatives to be a part of the association.

But wherever possible—without compromising his convictions or being identified with a policy not in keeping with those convictions—the pastor will find it advantageous and profitable to his work to be a part of the ministers' association.

Cooperation With Other Churches

There are many situations in which the pastor can lead his congregation in cooperation with churches of other denominations. Today's cooperative efforts advance the cause of Christ and enhance the spiritual lives of the believers. Such activities as city-wide evangelistic crusades and projects dealing with certain moral issues—for example, pornography, prostitution, and gambling—have the potential of preserving the community for good.

One of the first things ministers of the gospel should learn is that they are not in competition with other preachers. The mission is not to build bigger churches, to show a better record, to achieve more than others, or to be more popular. We must realize that "we be brethren" and together we have a mandate to "preach the gospel to all the world—to make disciples of all nations." We need each other to carry out that command.

In 1979 when I preached at the General Council of the Assemblies of God in Baltimore, I was introduced by a long-time friend, Roy Weed, who facetiously said, "Jim Hamill has pastored a church that for many years has been in first place in world ministries giving and in Sunday school attendance, but he must be losing ground. He was not in first place last year." When I stood to preach, I expressed my philosophy about competition in the work of God by saying, "It is true my church was not first in world missions giving last year. However, our church did give the largest amount in its history last year, but there were three or four churches that gave more! I hope that next year we give much more to world ministries than we gave last year, and that a thousand churches will give more than we do to get the gospel to the world."

Pastors should guard against becoming jealous or critical of a colleague or competitive with him for attention, members, the finest building, and the like. Love should control our attitude toward our fellow ministers. Jesus said, "By this shall all men know that ye are my disciples, if ye have love one to another" (John 13:35).

Proclaim the Word of God Faithfully and Publicly

Sometimes conformity is good. In many instances it is commendable to conform to our environment, to fit into the pattern, to be conventional, to be one of the crowd, to share the opinions of all the rest, to bring our behavior in line with the majority, to discipline ourselves to the narrow dimensions of the standard. There is some virtue in conforming, in avoiding differences, divisions, and dissension.

At other times, conformity is bad. Virtue lies in *not* conforming to the pattern, *not* going with the majority, *not* doing what everybody else does.

Worldliness is much more than some people seem to understand. It is more than short or long hair, more than makeup, more than a woman's dress, more than sporting events and games and other types of entertainment. It may include some of these things, but it is much more and much deeper than that.

The word *world* in Paul's admonition "Be not conformed to the world" means "world system." He is saying that followers of Jesus are not to conform to the world, not to think like the world, not to live like the world, not to be a part of the world.

It is this whole world system, this evil age, that Jesus prayed that we be not a part of. Even though we are in the world, we are not a part of this godless, Christless, lustful, selfish, proud, hypocritical, pleasure-crazed crowd.

Worldliness is our attitude toward this world system, our interest in it, our enslavement to it, our participation in it, our evaluation of it, our desire for it.

If we are to please God, we are not to be conformed to this world. We are not to bring our lives in tune with this world. Our plans, affections, interests, ambitions, thinking, pleasures, future, living, must be apart from this world system, this evil age that is without God.

An absolute essential to leadership in any area, church, or community is courage. It is impossible to be a good leader without being courageous. To fill a place of leadership, one must have definite convictions and solid courage.

The minister's relationship to the general public should be such that the community knows where he stands on the important issues, particularly those relating to faith and morals. The minister does not have to compromise his convictions or pull any punches in his preaching in order to be of service to his community.

A great many Americans still like men who have the courage of their convictions, who are not afraid to speak up and speak out on the issues of the day. They may not agree with you, but they will respect you.

On many occasions over the fifteen or sixteen years that I've served on the panel of a local television program, "What Is Your Faith?" I have found it necessary to speak out as forcefully as I could on certain issues dealing with morals or faith. Several of the other members of the panel are rather liberal in their theology and life-style.

It is surprising how many telephone calls and letters I have received over the years in which people said, "I do appreciate your stand on this issue. I believe you. In fact, I believe your position is sounder than the position of the man on the panel who represents my denomination."

The pastor does not need to apologize for his church, its doctrine, its fundamental position, or its Pentecostal stand. The pastor should endeavor to never offend people, but at the same time, never compromise a conviction to accommodate people.

In Memphis, all the charitable groups, a dozen or more, were organized in order not to duplicate their efforts and to assure meeting all needs possible. I was asked to give the invocation at their annual business meeting banquet. Just a few moments before the banquet, the president said to me he thought it would be unwise to use the name of Jesus in the invocation inasmuch as several members present did not believe in Jesus. I said to him, "Then you will have to get another boy. I don't know how to pray except in the name of Jesus." So he said, "All right, go ahead." I prayed in the name of Jesus. Would you believe that day I was elected president of that group!

A good pastor will not pull himself into a shell, isolate himself from the activities of his community and city. He and his church should be cooperative with the community and with the city in any kind of program of merit. If we pull ourselves into a shell and show no interest in our community apart from our church itself, then we cannot expect much cooperation from the community and city. Co-operation is a two-way street.

A good image to project is that the church can be counted on to do its part in any project that is for the advancement of the faith or the betterment of the community. When First Assembly opened its new church on North Highland Street, *The Commercial Appeal*, the morning newspaper, carried an editorial on the church, commending it for its ministry and its cooperation in various city and community projects. One line I remember particularly was, "Memphis has come to depend upon First Assembly, knowing that it will always do its part in any worthwhile project."

NOTES

[1]Thomas F. Zimmerman, ed., *And He Gave Pastors* (Springfield, MO: Gospel Publishing House, 1979), p. 371.

[2]Ibid., p. 401.

[3]Ibid., p. 400.

[4]Nolan B. Harmon, Jr., *Ministerial Ethics and Etiquette* (New York: Abingdon–Cokesbury Press, 1928), pp. 59, 61, 62.

[5]R. D. E. Smith, "The Preacher and Politics," *Advance* 20 (July 1984):6-7.

[6]Frank S. Mead, ed., *Reaching Beyond Your Pulpit* (Old Tappan, NJ: Fleming H. Revell Co., 1967), p. 123.

6

The Pastor:
Leadership Requirements

No church will ever become larger or more spiritual than its leaders, officers, and workers. If we are to have big churches, we must have big pastors—not big in the way the world measures bigness but big according to God's measurements, men and women who weigh 16 ounces to the pound and measure 36 inches to the yard.

The Bible is filled with men and women who are outstanding leaders. Some had one type of responsibility and some another, but all had one thing in common—they led people.

Leaders are not born, they are made. If you study Bible characters such as Joseph, Moses, and Gideon, you are impressed with the fact that they were not born leaders—they became leaders. They learned the skill of leadership.

Dr. Clyde M. Narramore singles out the starting point in developing leadership ability: "Give first place to deep spirituality." The leaders of the church must spiritually motivate their people.

The mission of the church, put very simply, is to worship God, build His church, and evangelize the world. The mission of the church leader, as we said before, is to develop and establish every believer by teaching and training him, thus building God's church. The church leader is to be a channel to lead God's people into a Spirit-filled life.

A leader then is a motivator. The pastor is to spiritually motivate his people. He must lead them into spiritual experiences with God. He must motivate them to live for God, work for God, worship God. He must motivate his staff and his volunteer workers. He must do this without the help of the promise of large salaries, significant promotions, or high honors.

While in college, our youngest son, Don, served on my staff for eighteen months. Later he applied for a sales job with a fairly large corporation. The sales manager asked for his experience in sales. Don told him that he had worked only at odd jobs except the eighteen months on his father's staff. Whereupon the sales manager said to him, "Well, then, you really have had no experience in sales. Preachers are not very good salesmen."

Don replied, "Sir, I do not wish to be disrespectful, but how many salesmen do you have who could get hundreds of people to come out every Sunday to hear their 'sales pitch'? I think preachers are excellent salesmen."

The sales manager grinned and said to him, "I believe you are right. I'll give you a job."

Dwight Eisenhower described leadership as "the act of getting somebody else to do something you want done because he wants to do it."

The Christian leader must use spiritual truths and good management skills to capture the imagination and energy of his coworkers. Peter Drucker in *The Practice of Management* calls this giving the staff member a managerial vision. In order to properly motivate coworkers, Drucker says they must sense the overall purpose and be convinced that their job properly done will be a valid contribution.[1]

The pastor must be the leader in the church's evangelistic and missionary endeavors. The church has a commission, "Go ye into all the world, and preach the gospel to every creature" (Mark 16:15) and "Make disciples of all nations" (Matthew 28:19, RSV). This is a mandate, a requirement, an order, a charge. In these words of our Lord, we have the original missionary impulse and imperative: the Great Commission.

This is our God-given commission. This must become our passion. This should be our magnificent obsession. For this purpose we came into the world, for this purpose we exist, for this purpose we are banded together as a church. While this is the mission of the universal Church, it is also the mandate of the local church.

In 1965, my wife Katheryne and I were on a missionary/preaching trip that took us to Kuala Lumpur, Malaysia. While we were there, the missionary, Jimmy Jones, requested that we assist him in securing a missionary evangelist who could spend several weeks in

Kuala Lumpur with the hope of establishing a Chinese church. We agreed, so upon our return to the States we asked Gene and Ruth Martin to go. Our church arranged to pay the total expense of the campaign.

At the conclusion of their meeting, enough people had come to Christ to establish a church. Gene proceeded to raise funds for the erection of a building. Our congregation again contributed several thousand dollars and others made contributions sufficient to build a church building. We never heard much about the church thereafter, except from time to time that the church in Kuala Lumpur was a good church.

In 1982, I again was preaching in the Far East, including Kuala Lumpur. I was delighted to discover that the church had some two thousand people on Sunday morning, had established eight branch churches, and had pledged to World Missions that year two hundred forty thousand American dollars!

If we had not taken a leadership role, the church in Memphis would have never known anything about the great need in Kuala Lumpur. We would have missed the glorious opportunity of sharing in the establishment of that church, which is a beacon throughout the Far East.

The pastor is the administrative leader of the church. He should acquaint himself with every activity of the church; all paid personnel should be accountable to him; all volunteer personnel should be approved by him; all meetings, speakers, musicians, participants, and all other activities should have his approval.

The pastor should know more about the financial condition of the church than any member of the board! He must assume a place of leadership in the church's financial affairs.

God has called all believers to service, but He has set aside some for ministerial leadership (1 Corinthians 12:28 and Ephesians 4:11). Those in positions of leadership are assigned the task of enlisting, coordinating, overseeing, supervising, and directing the total work of the church congregation.

The Pastor Must Have Character

A good dictionary definition of *character* is "a composite of good moral qualities, typically of moral excellence and firmness blended with resolution, self-discipline, high ethics, force and judgment."

Ministry without character of this kind is just so much religious activity—religious business, if you please. For this, Jesus condemned the Pharisees. More interested in the praise of men than in the approval of God, more concerned about reputation than about character, the Pharisees succeeded only in achieving hypocrisy.

According to Owen Carr, we run the same risk today: "Too often we are concerned with *reputation*, when God's concern is *character*. If we take care of character, reputation will take care of itself." Carr goes on to say, "It is possible to develop character. This is evidenced throughout the Scripture, as well as in modern examples. Since character can be developed, it is important that we pay particular attention to this phase of our life. . . . Nothing so changes, enhances, and beautifies human character as an intimate and proper relationship with God."[2]

C. I. Scofield amplifies the matter: "Christian character is not mere moral or legal correctness, but the possession and manifestation of nine graces: love, joy, peace—character as an inward state; longsuffering, gentleness, goodness—character in expression toward man; faith, meekness, temperance—character in expression toward God. Taken together they present a moral portrait of Christ."[3]

Dr. Zenas Bicket points out, however, that "one careless slip of personal conduct can destroy in a moment that which has taken years of diligent effort to build."[4] Pastors as leaders must guard against many insidious things that will destroy their ministry. A few of these include love for money, love of applause, familiarity with the opposite sex, discouragement, and pride.

Pride is a heart problem. And although it does not always arise from external sources, a pastor given excessive exaltation, special honors, large and frequent gifts, and placed on a pedestal can easily become the victim of pride. Many of the problems in pastoral leadership are rooted in pride—pride of person and pride of position. Proverbs 16:10 is a solemn warning: "Pride goeth before destruction."

Some people seem to think that to become humble is to become weak, that meekness is weakness, but God said that Moses (perhaps the greatest leader of all time) was the meekest man upon the earth (Numbers 12:3). There is certainly no evidence that Moses was ever weak. Humility provides a strength of character that comes from no other source.

Once in a meeting of the General Presbytery when I was complimented for something, someone teasingly remarked, "He really likes that. He is very humble, and it will not affect him."

I facetiously responded, "Brethren, I know that there are many preachers who are better preachers than I. I am certain that there are many pastors who do a much better job pastoring than I, and that there are many administrators who do a better job than I, but when it comes to humility, I am at the top of the list."

As leaders we must not take ourselves too seriously. That is often the opposite of humility.

The Pastor Must Have Vision

A leader has a vision that usually extends further than the average person's. He looks not only at today, he gets a glimpse of tomorrow. The leader sees not only immediate goals, he projects long-term goals. And he knows how to attract people to his vision.

Men with a vision are positive men and the masses will follow them. People are always attracted to something that is moving, dynamic, and full of life. A church, a program, or a cause that is going somewhere and a leadership that knows where it is going will always attract people.

Men who have blessed the world, whether in science, medicine, statesmanship, economics, Christianity, or in any other field, have been men with vision.

Someone wrote, "The world has been saved by its madmen." Columbus, Samuel B. Morse, Cyrus Field, Marconi, the Wright brothers, Alexander Graham Bell, Robert Fulton, were all in their day called madmen, but they were men who had a vision.

While touring Africa some years ago, again and again I came across the effects of the life of David Livingstone. Men traced Caesar's march through Gaul by the villages he destroyed, the fields he devastated, and the homes he burned; but we trace Livingstone's progress through Africa by the desert places that became gardens and wildernesses that became pools of water.

Livingstone was born in poverty and worked in the mills of Scotland as a child. With the first crown he earned, he bought a Latin grammar. He heard God's call to Africa, and he spent twenty-five years in the heart of that dark continent. In two years, Livingstone had twenty-seven attacks of fever lasting from one to three weeks, but it was the vision of this man that opened up Africa to missions.

Mediocre men are never men of vision.

Disraeli is quoted as having said, "It is a wretched thing to be gratified with mediocrity when the excellent lies before us."[5]

The spirit of mediocrity has manifested itself today in lighthearted unconcern and shameful shirking of duty. Unfortunately we have developed a philosophy in this nation that serves mediocrity: Do as little as you can, work as little as you can, study as little as you can, go to church as little as you can, pray as little as you can. Don't ever go beyond the call of duty—don't go the second mile.

Frank Crain in a sweeping indictment of the mediocre wrote, "Most preachers you hear are bad—not bad men, but bad preachers. Most singers cannot sing. Most actors are mediocre. Most teachers are poor teachers. Most books are a waste of time. . . . Most cooks cannot cook."[6]

Not only has this curse of mediocrity touched our scientific, economic, and educational world, but it has invaded professing Christendom. Such Christians have plenty of sentiment but make no sacrifice; when a piano is to be moved, they escape by carrying the bench.

Owen Meredith describes these people in these lines: "Down the path of life that led nowhere he trod./Where his whims were his guides,/And his will was his god,/And his pastime his purpose."[7]

Some other more familiar lines could also be applied: "Solomon Grundy, born on Monday, christened on Tuesday, married on Wednesday, took ill on Thursday, worse on Friday, died on Saturday, buried on Sunday, and that was the end of Solomon Grundy." That is mediocrity.

Many of God's people have been content to think in terms of conventional Christianity; comfortable and smug, they have no sense of conquest or ambition for great things. I was rather amused on one occasion when the famous Pastor Robert G. Lee preached at First Assembly. He described what he called the "Bantam Baptists," the "Midget Methodists," the "Pygmie Presbyterians," the "Little Lutherans," and the "Easygoing Episcopalians." My congregation was in 100-percent agreement until he mentioned the "Puny Pentecostals." The church of Jesus Christ so vitally needs leaders who are mature men, strong-willed with clear visions, men who are not afraid to be different, who will lead the people out of complacency and mediocrity.

The pastor must assume the responsibility of leading the people out of doubts and fears and misgivings, out of the fog of unbelief into the sunlight of God's victory. After all, we represent a triumphant Christ and we are members of the Church that He built—a Church that the gates of hell shall not prevail against.

The Pastor Must Have Courage

As was pointed out in chapter 5, another essential in leadership is courage. It is impossible to be a good leader without being courageous. To fill a place of leadership one must have definite convictions and the courage to live by them.

When God called Joshua to succeed Moses as the leader of Israel, He repeatedly told this new leader, "Be strong and of good courage" (Joshua 1:6,7,9).

The disciples, before they became founders of the New Testament church, needed courage. Before Pentecost they had not taken a place of leadership in their communities or made an impact upon the towns in which they lived. They all ran away in the Garden of Gethsemane. Peter denied the Lord, and after the crucifixion and burial of Jesus, they were all hiding behind closed doors. Then the Holy Spirit came upon them. He filled their hearts and hurled them out into the streets. Their once silent voices were blaring out like trumpets. Rome demanded, "Be silent," but they replied, "Woe to us if we preach not the gospel, for we cannot but preach what we have seen and heard." And so they "filled all Jerusalem with their doctrine"; they had become courageous leaders through the agency of the Holy Spirit.

The Pastor Must Have Wisdom

Jesus told His disciples they were to be "wise as serpents, and as harmless as doves" (Matthew 10:16).

The Lord also promised, "If any of you lack wisdom, let him ask of God, that giveth to all men liberally" (James 1:5). God has provided the Church with the gift of wisdom.

I cannot overemphasize how tremendously important it is that leaders have and use great wisdom in dealing with people. Wisdom to properly evaluate, wisdom to organize, wisdom to enlist others for the Kingdom, wisdom to assign responsibilities, wisdom in dealing with people.

Dealing with people requires the wisdom often called common sense. Someone has said that "common sense is that sense without which all other sense is nonsense." The pastor must wisely deal with the members of his congregation. He must deal with them individually. No set formula can be applied to each situation that develops in a church. Wisdom must dictate the decision.

Almost forty years ago, when I first went to Memphis as pastor, there was a man in the church who had been saved only a short time. Stanley McRae at the time of his conversion was a professional heavyweight prizefighter with the promise of a successful career.

However, McRae felt he could not pursue such a career. He resigned from the ring, came to Memphis, and went to work at the Ford motor plant. Well known as a prizefighter and very enthusiastic as a Christian, he attracted the attention of many of the men with whom he worked. They teased him, calling him "preacher," but for the most part respected him.

However, one man took advantage of the situation; by his practical jokes and slurs, he made life rather miserable for this new Christian. One day the man made the mistake of pretending to strike the former prizefighter. Stanley McRae's reflexes were such that he reacted with a real punch that knocked the bully cold! When the boxer realized what he had done, he quickly picked the man up, put him in his own car, and drove him to the hospital. Then he went next door and bought the man some flowers, after which he came by the church to talk to me about what he had done.

While deep in my heart I felt that the bully got what he deserved, I explained to McRae that God would forgive him. We had prayer together and he left my office very happy. Needless to say, he had no more problems at work. I believe it was wisdom to pray with him and encourage him, rather than to say, "I don't blame you, I would have socked him too."

A pastor has to be patient with people but wise enough not to allow disagreements to become issues. We erected a building where I pastored before going to Memphis. The church board wanted to put a kitchen in the new church, but there was a very vocal group in the congregation who objected to kitchens in churches. (Those were the days before we had banquets, luncheons, and dinners at hotels. It was necessary to entertain all sectional, district, and regional eating meetings at the church.) I suggested to the board that we not antagonize those folk, but rather plan for the space, rough in the plumbing, the electricity, and the like, and let me handle it from there. I appointed the most vocal of the antikitchen group to the entertainment committee. It wasn't long until they were suggesting we should have provided a kitchen in the new church. I said, "I believe you're right. I'll see what we can do about it." We never had any more kitchen problems.

Many years ago we had in the church an elderly couple, Mr. and Mrs. Frank Morton. Mr. Morton was in very poor health and retired. They attended church together, went to the grocery store together, prepared meals together, and washed dishes together. They were inseparable. One day Mr. Morton died suddenly of a heart attack. A neighbor telephoned the church. I was out of the office at the time, so an assistant went immediately to the Morton home. A few minutes later he called the church secretary and asked her to find me and have me come at once to the Morton's home.

When I arrived, the undertaker was in the yard. He said, "I am so glad you are here." The assistant pastor was standing on the porch. His first remark to me was, "They didn't teach me in Bible school what to do in a situation like this."

Mrs. Morton had gone into shock; she would not let them touch the body. She was saying, "God is too good to take my husband from me. He is not dead. God knows how much we love each other and how much we need each other." I talked with her as you would talk to a little girl, telling her that when God had saved Mr. Morton some fifty years ago, He claimed priority on his life. He had been so good to leave Mr. Morton with her for all these years, and now He wanted him to come and live with Him, and someday He would call for her to join them in heaven. Like a child, she understood and agreed that "the Lord doeth all things well."

As a pastor I learned that we deal with different and sometimes difficult situations almost daily. Therefore, we must constantly pray for wisdom to deal with each need as it arises.

The Pastor Must Have Faith

Faith is essential to good leadership. No person can be a successful pastor without faith, without preaching faith, without teaching his people to have faith: "Without faith it is impossible to please [God]" (Hebrews 11:6).

"The broadest definition of Biblical faith is that confidence in God which leads us to active trust in Him. . . . Any really useful definition of faith must include confidence in the Holy Scriptures as the authoritative word of God. Very simply put, faith is taking God at His word and acting on it" (Scofield).

In material things, "seeing is believing." In the spiritual, "believing is seeing." Jesus said, "If thou wouldest believe, thou shouldest see the glory of God" (John 11:40). The pastor must preach and teach the people that we are saved by faith, kept by faith, healed by faith, and that our prayers are answered through faith. But there are two kinds of faith the preacher should be aware of: superficial faith and special faith. The pastor as a leader of the people must be able to determine the difference between the two.

The definition of superficial is "concerned only with the obvious and apparent, not profound, shallow, not penetrating the surface, not significant, not genuine, external, exterior, on the surface."

In Philip's great revival in Samaria we have an example of superficial faith in the case of Simon the Sorcerer. "Simon himself believed also: and . . . was baptized" (Acts 8:13).

That Simon became a believer of a certain type cannot be denied. He declared his faith in the doctrine Philip preached. He identified himself with the disciples. As we might say today, he joined the church and was baptized.

It is, nevertheless, obvious that Simon was concerned with only the externals. He had no change of heart. We read that he continued with Philip and wondered at the miracles and signs. Simon believed, but it was more a gesture than anything else. Instead of being moved by repentance for sin and a supreme desire for the power and the fellowship of the Lord, his action was dictated by enthusiasm over signs and wonders and eagerness to traffic in them.

It was a "sign-supported faith," which Jesus plainly warned against.

Some people today are like Simon. They believe in miracles. They no doubt believe that God performs the miracles—but they are not willing to accept the Lord Jesus as the Lord and Master of their lives. This was illustrated to me during the first Oral Roberts campaign in Memphis in 1950: People actually stole the prayer cards to get into the healing line.

Jesus wants us to believe in Him as Lord and Saviour, not just as a miracle worker. Real saving faith must pass beyond the physical evidence of Him who gave it. It must stop at nothing short of a deep, humble, penitent, personal trust in the divine character and redemptive claims of Jesus Christ.

Please do not construe what I have said to mean that I do not believe in miracles or that I am discouraging the preaching of faith that brings miracles. I am a miracle. First, a miracle of God's grace and, second, a miracle of God's healing power when three doctors thought I was going to die with a cancer of the lung. We must preach a faith that is rooted and grounded in God's inerrant Word and a faith that is in Jesus Christ, emphasizing what He does in us spiritually rather than physically.

This is the type of faith we must preach if we expect to build the church of Jesus Christ. In John 6:26-40, 66, we see the multitudes forsake Jesus. They believed, at least to a degree, for they had followed Him for the fishes and the loaves and to behold the miracles that He did.

But when Jesus laid down the principles of the Kingdom, they left Him. Why? Because they had no conviction of sin, no desire to forsake evil, no real love for God, no real devotion to Jesus. They believed, but they refused to accept and receive the Lord Jesus Christ. Pastors must be aware of the fact that it is possible to have a superficial faith in a creed or an institution, a faith that does not include the Christ of that creed or the Christ of that institution.

Some church members are fundamental in their belief. They have no questions or doubts about the deity of Christ, the authority of the Word of God, or the importance of the church. They believe the Bible, they believe in the institution of the church, they believe the doctrines of some particular denomination; yet their faith is simply in a creed rather than in Christ as their Saviour.

It is possible to have a superficial faith in tradition and in a code of ethics, both founded by Jesus Christ, without having a personal faith in Jesus Christ himself.

This explains the multiplied thousands who join the church and are good people so far as their behavior, character, and relationships are concerned. They assume they are Christians. But they have not personally encountered Jesus Christ. He has not dealt with the sin problem in their hearts. They have never had the joy of hearing Him say, "Thy sins be forgiven thee." They have not been regenerated, they have not been born again.

If in our preaching the emphasis is on the superficial, then those to whom we preach will believe in the superficial. If we put the emphasis on the institutions and traditions, on the sensational, on the fishes and loaves, the people will believe in those things, rather than in Jesus Christ the Son of God.

There is a superficial faith, but thank God, there is a real faith, a saving, keeping, healing, miracle-working faith.

Now special faith goes beyond this, outside the usual channel and scope of ordinary faith. Special faith believes without specific promises or precedents. Special faith believes because of confidence and faith in the goodness and the faithfulness of God.

The mother of Jesus, Mary, told Him there was no more wine at the wedding of Cana. She did not know what He would do. She did not know what could be done. But she knew He could, and believed He would, do something about it—that was special faith.

The Syrophoenician woman came to Jesus and asked that an unclean spirit be cast out of her daughter. She was requesting something to which she was not entitled by law or by tradition as a Gentile. Until Jesus died for the whole world she had no scriptural claim of healing for her daughter. But she had faith in the goodness, mercy, concern, and faithfulness of God. And it resulted in her daughter's healing.

Special faith believes God for things we have not experienced before, have not specifically been promised in the Bible, or have not known of other people to receive.

Special faith takes five loaves and two fishes and feeds five thousand. Special faith feeds a prophet from an empty cruse of oil. Special faith uses ravens to feed a prophet.

Hebrews 11 is a record of special faith: "By faith Abel . . . ," "by faith Enoch . . . ," "by faith Noah . . . ," "by faith Abraham . . . ," and on and on it goes. When I was just a boy preacher, I was invited to preach in Columbia, Tennessee. It had no full-gospel church. As a matter of fact, a full-gospel meeting had never been held in that little city. Four women who moved there from another town had prayed many years for a church. (Their husbands were not Christians.) A preacher in Nashville heard about them and came to Columbia to meet them. They decided to secure a tent and invite me for a meeting of four weeks' duration, hoping to start a church.

When I arrived, I learned they had spent all their money before they had arranged for seating in the tent. I was told that the University of Tennessee Experiment Station had some excellent chairs. I went to see the manager and asked him to loan us four hundred chairs. I did not ask to rent them, but to borrow them!

Even though that's been more than fifty years ago, I can still remember that distinguished, gray-haired man looking across his desk and saying, "Mr. Hamill, we have never allowed other people to use our equipment and furnishings."

I replied, "Mr. Porter, this is an experiment station, isn't it?"

He looked at me in surprise and, I think, shock for a full thirty seconds before he grinned and said, "It certainly is, and I am going to loan you those chairs." (That was special faith, for I had no specific guiding Scripture passage or precedent.)

Alexander the Great conquered the known world and marched until he came to the great Himalaya Mountains. The Greeks had made a map of the world, but it included only the world they knew.

Alexander commanded an officer to study the map and tell him where they were. The officer consulted the map and returned to report, "Sir, I have studied the map and as far as I can see we have marched off the map. We are now in uncharted world."

So it is with the pastor who has special faith and preaches special faith—he can lead his people into an uncharted world with God. He can teach them to become more than conquerors, to not only conquer the known spiritual territory, but territory not yet mapped. He can lead off the map of fear and doubt and unbelief into a life of victory.

NOTES

[1]Terry Muck, "How I Motivate My Staff," *Leadership* 1 (Summer 1980):81.

[2]Thomas F. Zimmerman, ed., *And He Gave Pastors* (Springfield, MO: Gospel Publishing House, 1979), pp. 65, 66, 67.

[3]C. I. Scofield, ed., *Scofield Reference Bible* (New York: Oxford University Press, 1917), p. 1247.

[4]Zenas J. Bicket, comp. and ed., *The Effective Pastor* (Springfield, MO: Gospel Publishing House, 1973), pp. 4, 10.

[5]Robert G. Lee, *Bread From Bellevue Oven* (Wheaton, IL: Sword of the Lord Publishers, 1947), p. 132.

[6]Ibid.

[7]Ibid., p. 138.

7

The Pastor:
His Morals, Morale, and Money

A godly life is the first requirement of the pastor and the final benediction of his ministry. The first qualification listed for a bishop in 1 Timothy 3:2 is that he "must be blameless." The personal life of the pastor cannot be separated from a godly life. Without a godly life, it makes little difference what he says.

There is a difference between character and reputation. Character is what you really are, what God knows you to be, and reputation is what people think you are. But the truth is, over a reasonable period of time, people think you to be what you really are.

Our behavior as representatives of God, as ambassadors for Christ, is very important. We are admonished to walk circumspectly before all men. We are told that we are "epistles read and known of all men."

"He is a good man" is the highest compliment one can pay his pastor. I have often said when my family and friends stand beside my grave, I would rather that they would be able to say he was a good man than to say he was a great preacher, a wise leader, a good administrator, or anything else.

In Acts 11:24, Barnabas was described as "a good man, and full of the Holy Ghost and of faith." I believe a significant part of that verse is the last clause: "and much people was added unto the Lord." I believe that because of Barnabas' fullness of the Spirit and because of his goodness many people were added to the Lord.

The Pastor's Obligation to Duty

Pastors are placed in a unique position so far as their obligations are concerned. They are not asked to punch a time clock, give a written report of their activities, or account to any person or persons in particular as to how they spend their time.

Pastors do not record the time they spend visiting and counseling people, or the hours they spend praying, studying, and preparing. Now, all of these things are reflected in a pastor's ministry and in the success of his work. If he does not fulfill his obligations, he does not succeed in the work of God.

It is morally wrong for a man to accept a position as pastor and the salary of a pastor and not, to the best of his ability, fulfill that responsibility. Even though the pastor does not have a boss or a supervisor or a time clock, he has an obligation; his character will determine how he fulfills that obligation.

It is impossible for a pastor to fulfill his duties and at the same time "fiddle away his days." He cannot usually sleep until mid-morning, leisurely read the morning newspaper while drinking his coffee, play golf, go fishing, take his wife shopping, and visit with fellow ministers.

Although it is necessary for the pastor to have some type of recreation and some time of rest, and although it is possible to sin against the body and against God by not setting aside time for these things, I sincerely believe that more preachers are underworked than overworked.

Some years back a newspaper reporter telephoned me for my opinion about a report that a number of the larger denominations had declined in membership. My reply was, "A misplaced emphasis in the pulpit and complacency in the pew." Pastors must learn to evaluate, to know what is important, what is paltry, what is major, what is minor, what is primary, what is secondary. Many fail in the ministry or are defeated in life because of their choices. They major in minors.

In 1 Kings 20 the prophet relates the parable of a man who allowed his prisoner to escape. His superior had left a prisoner with him and told him to guard the prisoner with his life. When the superior returned and asked the soldier where the prisoner was, the soldier replied, "While I was busy here and there, he was gone." This story could very easily be the picture of a pastor who is extremely busy here and there doing things in general and nothing in particular.

Pastors need to practice self-discipline in establishing priorities, working energetically and enthusiastically at the task that is theirs: prayer, the study of the Word, the preparation for preaching and teaching, counseling, and witnessing. The pastor's character will determine how he spends his time, how he fulfills his obligations.

The Pastor's Integrity

Lewis B. Smedes says, "Personal integrity in a minister is an indispensable quality, yet it comes only with great struggle. . . . Dulling the cutting edge of honesty is really very easy. Masks get comfortable very soon. Roles are learned terribly fast. Ministerial cosmetics go on quickly. A pastor who keeps to basics will earn respect and trust over the long haul, while the magnetic, smooth-talker fumbles his way to another [pastorate]."[1]

The first priority of the pastor is the responsibility of his own personal life. As a spokesman for God to the people and as a representative of the people before God, he must be a man of integrity, preserving a blameless reputation before his people.

In one sense, integrity is a matter of wholeness, soundness. To have integrity means one is not divided within himself—trying to serve two masters, being double-minded. The opposite of integrity is hypocrisy, duplicity. "The voice is Jacob's voice, but the hands are the hands of Esau" (Genesis 27:22, NKJV).

Roy C. Price says, "God commands us to be holy. Since holy means 'to be whole,' it is a synonym for integrity. Moral wholeness means keeping our promises, being honest in all personal and business transactions and maintaining moral purity."[2] Such things as keeping appointments, doing exactly what we say we will do when we say we will do it, fulfilling our commitments, meeting our obligations financially—such matters make up integrity.

The Pastor Must Be Ethical

The pastor must be ethical with his congregation, his fellow ministers, his denomination, and his community.

Ethics is defined as "the science of human duty or the principles of right action." An example of ethical conduct on the part of the pastor is the keeping of confidences. "Confidences entrusted to the pastor should be shared with no one who is not professionally involved with a person's care. As a rule, even the minister's spouse should not have access to them. A pastor's reputation for keeping or breaking confidences is readily available among his members."[3] If he is to maintain the proper relationship of pastor to member, in which the member shares with him needs and problems, the pastor must respect that confidence and not share it with other people.

In the relationship with fellow ministers, the pastor should be conscious of the ethical code that governs conversation. It is unethical to criticize other clergymen. We should strive at all times to build confidence in the ministry and to teach the people to hold clergymen in the highest esteem. It is also unethical to criticize one member of the church to another. Gossip and criticism must be avoided if we are to exemplify for our people the right attitude toward God and God's people.

The following is a partial list of unethical practices compiled by Lowell Ashbrook.

"1. Showing excessive attention toward members visiting from another assembly.

"2. Enticing members of another church by giving them a . . . position after they have visited your services.

"3. Accepting members of a neighboring church without contacting the pastor.

"4. Entering into conversation that is critical of a fellow minister.

"5. Taking advantage of a fellow minister's pulpit to preach things controversial or to promote oneself.

"6. Working against a host pastor's best interests, either among the members or from the pulpit, while serving as an evangelist.

"7. Failing to work in complete harmony with the elected pastor while holding membership in a local church as a minister.

" 'And as ye would that men should do to you, do ye also to them likewise' (Luke 6:31). This Biblical command sums up the guidelines for practicing good ministerial ethics."[4]

The Pastor's Disposition

The minister's disposition is important because it is usually reflected in his congregation. After a reasonable period of time, at least to a large extent, the attitude of the congregation becomes the same as the pastor's.

Magnanimous

The pastor should manifest a magnanimous spirit. God has provided different ways of getting His truth across to us. In the New Testament, for example, we have history to inform us, doctrine to instruct us, and examples to inspire us.

Among the Bible's examples of magnanimity is Barnabas. In Acts 9 we see Barnabas befriending Saul of Tarsus, in Acts 11 Barnabas is involved in the development of an ongoing New Testament church, in Acts 13 he and Paul are the first missionaries, and in Acts 15 we see Barnabas endeavoring to help a young, struggling preacher. What a beautiful example for all preachers.

Barnabas was a pastor with a magnanimous spirit, especially where people were concerned. In Acts 9 we have the story of the conversion of Saul of Tarsus, who had been notorious for his opposition to the Christian cause—tireless and relentless in his persecution of the Christians. Paul is converted on the Damascus Road and begins to witness for Christ. He then journeys down to Jerusalem and wants to be received into the fellowship of the Christians, but they are afraid of him. When he attempts to join the disciples, they are all suspicious of him. They hold him at arm's length.

We read, "But Barnabas took him" (Acts 9:27). He brought Paul to the apostles and declared to them how, on the road, Paul had met the Master, been converted, and had been boldly preaching Jesus in Damascus. Here was a magnanimous soul who wasn't going to keep a new convert out of the fellowship or be unforgiving toward him because he had been so cruel to the Christians.

Sometimes we Christians are so evangelical in our theology, so enameled in our sympathy, so hard and unforgiving toward people who have sinned, that we are more like the unforgiving servant in Jesus' parable than we are like Barnabas. Barnabas was bighearted in his treatment of a man who needed acceptance and couldn't get it. Barnabas was also generous and considerate toward John Mark, who failed miserably, but who came back and wanted to try again.

Barnabas was magnanimous in his dealing with the Gentile Christian movement beginning at Antioch. Many had turned to the Lord and "news of this came to the ears of the church in Jerusalem, and they sent Barnabas to Antioch. When he came and saw the grace of God, he was glad" (Acts 11:22, NASB).

An awkward situation arose at Antioch; some of the believers were Jews who had confessed Christ as the Messiah and Saviour, and some were Gentiles. Tensions and problems existed between Jews and Gentiles.

It was into this awkward situation that the Jerusalem leaders said, "Barnabas, you go. You have a ministry with these people." He wasn't an apostle, but they knew Barnabas had the right spirit. So he went to Antioch, and because of that magnanimous spirit he was able to minister to this mixed congregation.

In Antioch, Barnabas realized the program and the work were too big for one man, so he sought help. We are told, "A large company was added to the Lord. So Barnabas went to Tarsus to look for Saul" (Acts 11:24,25, NASB).

Don't overlook the significance of this situation. A smaller man would not have sought for an assistant. He, perhaps, would have said, "I'm going to be a big duck in a little puddle. I've got this all to myself. It's going to be *my* proposition, it's going *my* way, and I'm going to keep it that way."

Barnabas wanted to get the best man he could as an assistant, so he chose a first-class scholar, steeped in the Old Testament, well-read in philosophy, and now, above all, a follower of Christ. He said, "Paul is the man to cope with the difficulties and the possibilities that belong to this situation at Antioch. I will stand by him and hold up his hand, and we will work this out together."

Don't be too vocal with your fundamentalism, don't be too loud about your evangelicalism, don't be too proud of your so-called holiness if at the same time you have such a mean, cramped heart that you must have the limelight for yourself.

Enthusiastic

The pastor should be enthusiastic in his work. If you want an enthusiastic congregation, you must show some enthusiasm yourself. Enthusiasm is contagious. If you allow circumstances and conditions in your city and your church to defeat you, or cause you to take a defeatist attitude in your preaching or ministry in the church, your congregation will become defeated.

The pastorate provides the occasion for great spiritual successes and victories. To see God's work go forward and people come to

Christ, to be a part of the church's growth and the maturing of the believers, brings great joy to a pastor. Many things are discouraging to a pastor: when dreams, plans, and visions fail to materialize, when individuals fall by the wayside, when the church is not growing as rapidly as it should, and when the congregation appears to be complacent and unconcerned. These represent a real temptation to become disheartened.

But the pastor must lead his people with faith, courage, and assurance. I can recall on many occasions—when things were not going just the way I wanted them to, when things were not being accomplished that I had prayed and worked to accomplish—saying to the Lord, "Father, this is Your church. It is not mine. You sent me here. I am only Your servant trying to do what I believe You want me to do. Victory will be Yours."

To overcome discouragement pastors must be Biblically grounded, spiritually oriented, and divinely convinced that God has called, anointed, ordained, and commissioned them—that they are working in His will to accomplish His eternal purpose.

Joyful

Pastors should be joyful and cheerful in the work of God. There is great strength in joy. The Scriptures tell us, "The joy of the Lord is your strength" (Nehemiah 8:10). Any man who is trying to do the work of the Lord without the joy of the Lord will indeed be miserable and an unprofitable servant. Joy is the key to personal survival and to an effective and fruitful ministry. Pastors carry heavy responsibilities; they need the strength the joy of the Lord provides.

Pastors should not be guilty of the attitude manifested by the old lady when somebody asked her how she was feeling. She replied, "I always feel the worst when I feel the best because I know how bad I'm going to feel when I start feeling bad again."

Paul, in a Roman prison, not certain of his life (in fact, expecting it would soon end), wrote the epistle to the Philippians—a theme of which is rejoicing, being joyful. "Rejoice in the Lord always: and again I say, Rejoice" (Philippians 4:4).

Loving

The pastor should manifest a spirit of love. Dr. Warren W. Wiersbe says, "Apart from love, gifts and talents are hindrances to ministry. They become weapons, not tools. They exalt the servant, they do not edify the church. We may know little about the intricacies of communications theory . . . but if we love our people and serve them in love, we will somehow build bridges instead of walls, and our message will get across.

"Ministry is too sacred to be motivated by gain and too difficult to be motivated by duty. Only love can sustain us. . . . Only love makes a servant put others first. Only love keeps a servant from exploiting and using his people for his own purposes. Only love prevents a leader from becoming a dictator. Duty becomes a delight when it is saturated with love.

"But this love must not be manufactured. If it is, then it is not really love; it is shallow sentiment or cheap flattery. Rather, the fruit of the Spirit is love. 'God has poured out His love in our hearts by the Holy Spirit which He has given us' (Romans 5:5). Paul's own ministry was 'compelled by the love of Christ' (2 Corinthians 5:14), and it was this compassion-compulsion that helped to keep him going when things were difficult.

"Jonah ministered without love. He went to Nineveh, not because he loved God's will or the people to whom God had sent him, but because he feared God's chastening. The Elder Brother (Luke 15:25) labored dutifully in the field, but he had no love for either his father or his brother. Both men accomplished their work, but they missed the blessing. They ended up critical and divisive, unable to get along with God or men."[5]

Serving

The pastor must manifest the spirit of a servant. The person who does not want to work and serve others or the person who wants to enjoy center-stage attention with all the spotlights on him shouldn't enter the ministry. In the Early Church, the minister was a servant, not simply an officer. This concept was a novelty to the Greeks and Romans who considered a servant to be an unimportant nobody who did things for those who *were* important. Jesus Christ elevated and dignified service when He said, "I am among you as one who serves" (Luke 22:27, NIV).

Our society evaluates a man's worth by the number of people

who work for him. Jesus reversed that: "If anyone wants to be first, he must be the very last, and the servant of all" (Mark 9:35, NIV). The big question in ministry then is, How many people do you work for?

"This does not mean," writes Wiersbe, "that [the pastor] becomes a chore-boy for the . . . congregation. Ministry is not catering. Paul explained the difference when he wrote, '. . . ourselves as your servants for Jesus' sake' (2 Corinthians 4:5, NIV). First of all, we serve the Lord; sometimes that service must run counter to the ideas and desires of men. 'Am I now trying to win the approval of men, or of God?' Paul asked the critical Galatian believers. 'If I were still trying to please men, I would not be a servant of Christ' (Galatians 1:10, NIV).[6]"

Richard Dresselhaus says, "The pastor is first a servant of Jesus Christ. But he is also a servant of those to whom he is called to minister the life of Christ. Any man who is not prepared to be a servant dare not claim obedience to the divine call. No man is so miserable as the man who has the responsibilities of a pastorate but does not care to be a servant. He will chafe under the heavy demands, the unreasonable expectations, the uncertainties of the pastorate as a vocation and the continual burden of knowing people are depending on him. A servant counts it all joy and a privilege, but only a servant can do that.

"Young men and women who are considering the ministry need to settle this matter of servitude as part of their response to the call of God on their lives. Is he or she prepared to accept a life-style that revolves around the Lord's work? Will the continual demands of people become a burden too heavy to bear once the novelty of a new pastorate has worn off? Does the will of God for His kingdom have a place of preeminence in the heart? Can criticism and rejection be borne with joy and peace? It is all a vital part of servitude!"[7]

It seems pastors sometimes think the church was built for their benefit and to serve them, rather than the pastor being called to serve the congregation. It might be well if a pastor, when accepting a church, would at least say to himself, "I do not own this church. It was not built to accommodate me and to serve me. But I have been called to serve my Lord and the congregation in this place."

Peace-Seeking

The pastor should show a positive and peaceful attitude. Many things in a pastorate can contribute to a negative attitude if the pastor is not at peace with God and at peace with himself. Sometime in their career, pastors will have opposition: if not to them personally, to their policies and programs; if not from the congregation, then from the community. Dealing with people often involves conflicts of interest, personality, and policy. It is vital that a pastor manifest a peaceful and a positive attitude in dealing with controversies, disagreements, and misunderstandings.

A year or two after my retirement at Memphis, a long-time member, now a member of the board of deacons, said to me, "The thing I appreciated most about your leadership as pastor was that we never had a church fight or split in your thirty-seven years."

My reply was, "We could have had many."

The pastor must never allow differences of opinions to become an issue. In a positive manner he goes about finding the solution rather than adding fuel to the explosive matter. If the pastor endeavors to deal with difficulties and different opinions with an aggressive, hostile spirit, he will add to the problem rather than solve it.

The pastor needs to earnestly seek God for wisdom. James tells us that if any man lack wisdom, let him ask of the Lord who giveth liberally. Paul refers to the gift of the "word of wisdom." The Lord has the word of wisdom, a discerning mind, a spiritual insight, for the leaders of His people.

You can have a doctorate in philosophy from Harvard or Yale and yet be very insensitive to the things of the Spirit. If you want to be wise (not in the worldly sense of being clever), if you want to be knowledgeable, discerning, in spiritual matters, get to know your Bible thoroughly. The spirit the pastor manifests must demonstrate the belief that the work of God is more important than the differences of people; in the beauty of God's grace the church will proceed to fulfill the eternal purpose.

Uncritical

The pastor must not become jealous or critical of a colleague. The ugly manifestations of jealousy are revealed in the way we criticize other people. Instead of looking for the best qualities in others, we exaggerate their weaknesses and run down their achievements. We seem to have the false idea that it builds us up if we tear someone else down. C. E. Colton says in *The Minister's Mission*, "Nothing is more insidious than ministerial jealousy and no refined frailty more despicable and none more fatal ultimately to both happiness and usefulness."[8]

Saul, the first king of Israel, was destroyed by the spirit of jealousy. It so possessed him that he could not rejoice in the victory of God because the victory was being wrought through David rather than himself. He dethroned himself and wrecked his life because he could not take second place gracefully.

The pastor who cannot conquer the spirit of jealousy will eventually destroy his own ministry and severely damage the work of God. "He that ruleth his spirit [is better] than he that taketh a city" (Proverbs 16:32). "He that hath no rule over his own spirit is like a city that is broken down, and without walls" (Proverbs 25:28).

One of the outstanding men in the New Testament, Andrew, a spiritual giant, seemed to play second fiddle most of the time, yet without a trace of criticism or jealousy.

Andrew played second fiddle, but not by choice. He had some very good reasons for expecting and desiring to be among the first of the apostles. He was one of the first to become a disciple. What right had James or John or Simon to be ahead of him? Andrew became a follower of Jesus before any of them.

It must have been exceedingly trying on Andrew to be introduced as "Simon Peter's brother." When Andrew is mentioned in John's Gospel, usually the introduction is qualified by saying, "Simon Peter's brother." It may have annoyed him, but he didn't show it.

Sometimes he may have thought of resigning and going back to fishing. He could have said to himself, "I'd rather be first in a little boat on the Sea of Galilee than second fiddle among the apostles." But he got the victory over that because he was committed to the work of God first and Andrew second.

Before becoming a follower of Jesus, Andrew had been closely identified with Peter, James, and John. As boys they had played together, attended the synagogue together, grown to manhood, become partners in the fishing business; now they were following Jesus together. Andrew, it seemed, had a right to expect to remain a member of this quartet.

But his expectations were doomed to disappointment. The other three made the "inner circle." On the important occasions, such as the raising of Jairus' daughter from the dead, on the mountain when Jesus conferred with Moses and Elijah, and in the Garden of Gethsemane when Jesus faced the cross, He took with Him, not Andrew, but Peter, James, and John.

All this put Andrew in a place of testing. His, I think, was the hardest place in the apostolic college. Because they had been so intimate it was hard for Andrew to see his brother and two closest friends forge ahead, leaving him behind. We are often less tempted to envy when a stranger wins the coveted prize than when it is won by an old friend.

But the pastor must realize greatness of position is no absolute guarantee of greatness of soul. Someone has said, "Pygmies will be pygmies still, though perched in the Alps." And, of course, a small position is no indication of a little soul.

Jesus said, "Many that are first shall be last, and the last shall be first." How foolish, therefore, to regard ourselves as inferior because we are called upon to play on the second team. All of us must play second fiddle part of the time; most of us play second fiddle all the time: on the athletic field, in the home, in the church, out in the big world. Few of us play a leading part.

It is a happy day when a pastor realizes his calling, mission, and objective is to do God's will for his own ministry, large or small. He then will be able to rejoice in the success of his fellowman.

Insecure feelings on the part of a pastor are often revealed in jealous reactions. I have a friend who is a good man and very talented, but he has difficulties in almost every pastorate because he is exceedingly insecure. If members of his congregation are especially talented and they rise to places of leadership in the church, he unfortunately feels that their ability reveals his inefficiency in certain areas. The pastor must realize that the church will never be any stronger than the lay people he develops and uses in advancing the work of God.

One pastor who resigned his church to do missionary evangelism did not plan to move for a few months. The new pastor came to see the former pastor, telling him that if he continued to live in town, the new pastor himself would resign the pastorate immediately. This attitude is that of an insecure person, too immature to be a pastor.

However, the former pastor should respect his successor as God's man. It would be most unethical for a former pastor to interfere in any manner with the work of the present pastor or to criticize the pastor or any decision he makes or policy he advocates.

When I resigned the pastorate after thirty-seven years, I publicly announced that my wife and I hoped to continue to live in Memphis and to worship at the church when in town, and the new pastor would also be our pastor. We hoped to number among our friends the members of the church, but we would have no advice or counsel on church matters for any board, committee, or individual—except the pastor, and then only if he requested it. We emphasized that we would not talk with anyone about anything having to do with the church or his personal life that should be discussed with the pastor. This position on my part and the magnanimous attitude of the new pastor have made our relationship most pleasant and, I believe, spiritually profitable for both of us and the church.

Content

The pastor should manifest a spirit of contentment. Philip, one of the first deacons (in Acts 6) and a very successful evangelist (in Acts 8), is an example of a minister who was sensitive and obedient to the will of God as a "big time evangelist" or just as a host to others. The final glimpse we have of Philip in Acts is of a thrilling career drawing to a quiet close.

Between Acts 8 and Acts 21:5 are two decades. How long Philip was engaged in activity on a scale comparable to the Samaritan campaign or how long he continued to be a roving evangelist we do not know. The one thing that seems clear, however, is that when we meet Philip again, in Acts 21, he is not engaged in a spectacular ministry. It seems that his ministry was confined largely to his own place of residence in Caesarea.

While Philip faded from prominence, he did not fade from obedience. Demas faded shabbily, tragically. He forsook Paul and the Lord. His defeat was the defeat of a disloyal soul. But the same obedience that took Philip from Jerusalem to Samaria, from Samaria to the desert, from the desert to a princely chariot, was still his holy habit when we last have a look at him. Let our popularity with others pass if only our loyalty to Jesus remains.

Philip faded from fame, but he did not fade from fruitfulness. Though perhaps old in years, and possibly infirm, Philip's ministry continued, particularly in his own children.

And something bigger than signs remain—that character of Christ's likeness, the hallmark of the saint. It is a beauty that vanquishes bitterness, a sweetness that surmounts sourness, a tranquility that tramps over turbulence. The mark of a saint is that when career glamour is utterly gone, the character glow shines on.

The Pastor and His Money

Many preachers have been falsely accused of preaching for money. I am always offended when I hear a person carelessly and irresponsibly make that accusation.

I recall a story about Robert G. Lee, pastor of the famous Bellevue Baptist Church in Memphis for thirty-one years. Some forty or fifty years ago, when salaries were of course much lower, Lee was preaching in Miami. He was the guest on one of those radio talk shows where people telephone in and talk to the guest. One lady asked, "Dr. Lee, is it true that some preachers preach for money? I am told that your church pays you $12,000 per year. Is that correct?" Whereupon Dr. Lee replied, "No, ma'am, that is not correct. My church pays me $17,500 per year, and I am worth every penny of it."

When we today look at the salaries and income of leaders in industry, entertainment, sports, and other fields, it is a travesty of values to criticize the salaries that most pastors receive.

The call to preach the gospel does not include an oath of poverty, despite a commitment that involves financial sacrifice and a realization that preaching is not likely to make one rich.

In 1928, preachers (with a few exceptions) were men who wore blue serge suits, the kind that get slick looking when they're a little old. Their shirts were frayed and sometimes their shoes had been worn too long. At that time I was a teenage boy who felt a divine call to preach the gospel. When I committed my life to God, I sincerely believed that all of my life I would wear blue serge suits. Thank God, however, I have never worn one!

If we face up squarely to the truth, there are many who preach for money, and some of them are only hirelings. Too often money is the deciding factor in where the preacher will preach, what church he will accept, whether or not he will stay in that area of ministry.

However, most preachers are worth more than they are paid. Few of our clergymen receive as much as they deserve. Nevertheless, some receive far more than they could have earned in other vocations. Someone once asked me if I felt that my church paid me what I was worth. My reply was, "I can't afford to work for what I am worth."

I do not believe that the salary should be the deciding factor in whether a man accepts a place of ministry. I still believe that God will supply the needs of a man who is faithfully committed to preaching the Word of God. I once made that statement in a pastor's seminar, whereupon a young preacher said, "It's easy for one with a fairly large church to say such things."

I then said to him, "It might be of interest to you to know that my total income for the first full year that I spent in full-time ministry, preaching every week, was $172. I made real progress in the second year. I earned $258. I didn't feel too bad about it. I more or less took it philosophically, saying, 'Poor preach, poor pay. If I ever learn to preach, maybe they'll pay me.'"

When I reminisce about those early days, I think of so many times that God miraculously supplied my needs. As boy preachers, Jesse Smith (an outstanding preacher who served as pastor of several very fine churches and later as the superintendent of the Georgia district) and I were conducting a meeting in a little town in western Alabama. We received an invitation to hold meetings in Mississippi, for one of the larger churches in the South at that time. Of course we were anxious to go and felt that the Lord wanted us to do so, so we wrote that we would come. However, when the day arrived for us to take the train to our new meeting, we did not have sufficient funds. They had received an offering for us in the service the night before, but when we counted it there were so many pennies in the collection that I was reminded of what Paul said: "Alexander the coppersmith had done me much harm."

We went to the railroad station the next day without sufficient funds to buy tickets, feeling that if God had called us, God would supply. Moments before the train arrived, a lady drove up to the little station beside the railroad track and said to me, "My husband, Dr. Rudner, and I were in the meeting last night, but we did not have any money with us to give in the offering, so the doctor wanted me to give you this," and handed me some bills.

Would you believe that it was just sufficient to buy two tickets to the town we had planned to go to! This is only one of the many times God met the need so that I might continue to preach His Word.

Whatever the pastor's salary is, he should be very careful to live within his income. He must not obligate himself beyond his ability to pay, thus bringing reproach upon the cause of Christ. Going into debt beyond the ability to pay is one of the besetting sins of many clergymen today, resulting in an ineffective ministry for them.

The Pastor and Church Money

In most churches, the pastor is responsible for the financial welfare of the church and the administration of its fiscal program. He should be very careful in handling church money. In fact, it would be much better if the pastor didn't handle money. If he is responsible for the financial program of the church, he can direct it without actually making purchases, paying bills, and so forth.

It may be necessary in a few cases, particularly in a pioneer church, for the pastor to actually handle the money: receive it, count it, make the necessary purchases for the church, and generally manage the financial affairs. But in most churches this should not be the practice. There is too much room for misunderstanding. Invariably, the people think more money is being received than they are told, and that money is being wasted.

In established churches, there should be authorized members who handle the money and expenditures and give detailed reports under the supervision of the pastor. The pastor should be the church's most knowledgeable man about its financial condition, its budget, and its expenditures. But he should so conduct fiscal affairs as to never bring his integrity into question.

Opportunities for the pastor to be "a little unethical" in handling church finances are numerous—receiving public offerings; receiving money privately; indicating what the offering is for; remuneration of visiting clergymen, musicians, and missionaries; and meeting the financial obligations of the church.

Raising an offering for which the purpose is concealed from contributors is unethical. It is hypocritical to raise money for a popular project and then direct the money to another area without disclosure. Pastors have also been known to announce that a love offering was being received for a visiting clergyman, musician, or missionary, then allow only a part of it to reach the ministering guest. This is unethical.

Many people identify the church with the pastor and on occasion will hand him money that they fully intend for some church ministry. The pastor may rationalize that it was intended for his personal use, saying, "They gave me this money and said, 'Use it where it's needed most,' and I need it more than anybody else." It is dishonest not to put the money where the people intended it to go.

Some financial embarrassments are simply matters of carelessness. For example, some pastors make financial commitments to missionaries that the church will support them. In some cases, the pastor is not authorized to make such a commitment. In other instances, he fails to inform the congregation. The commitment may be discontinued on some flimsy excuse or perhaps no excuse at all. (A missionary goes to the field for four years. He rightfully assumes that the commitments made to him are good for that length of time.) The pastor should record such commitments and have an understanding with the church that such commitments will be continued in the event he vacates the pastorate.

The pastor is responsible to lead his congregation in meeting all of the financial obligations of the church. The church should have a reputation for honesty. Every member of the business community knows if the church pays its bills. Paul said, "Provide things honest in the sight of all men" (Romans 12:17). The church, the corporate body, is just as responsible for meeting its obligations as is the individual. One of the highest compliments members of my congregation ever paid me as a pastor was, "Pastor, you taught us the real joy of giving to God through the church, and you taught us that the church's integrity should always be unquestioned." The church should take great pride in meeting all of its obligations when due.

I remember one time especially when it was rather difficult to meet all the obligations on the due date. We had erected a new church building. In our financial calculations was the selling of the old building, which did not occur as early as we had hoped and planned. I recall so vividly standing in my pulpit on the first Sunday morning of August 1962 and telling my congregation that during the month of August, in order to meet all obligations, we must have $21,500. I said to the congregation, "Now, I will not ask who will raise their hand, giving $1,000 or $100 or $10; I will not report on the second or third Sunday that *X* number of dollars has been given and we lack so much, but let us this month prove that God is with us. Let each of us do what we can and see God supply our needs."

When the offerings were totaled, we had received $21,528. I then said to the people, "In September we do not need that amount, but we do have to have $16,000 and we will proceed the same way." At the end of September, the offerings amounted to $16,078. For a third month we decided to show the people that God was in fact and indeed directing the affairs of His church; that month the goal was $17,000. Again the offering equaled the need: $17,250. Dealing with that many people and that many dollars over a period of three months and receiving almost the exact amount needed, nobody but nobody could ever tell that congregation that God was not leading His church to victory!

NOTES

[1]Roy C. Price, "Building Trust Between Pastor and Congregation," *Leadership* 1 (Spring 1980):50.

[2]Price, p. 48.

[3]Thomas F. Zimmerman, ed., *And He Gave Pastors* (Springfield, MO: 1979), p. 203.

[4]Ibid., p. 155.

[5]Warren Wiersbe, "Principles Are the Bottom Line," *Leadership* 1 (Winter 1980): pp. 82, 83-84.

[6]Ibid., p. 82.

[7]Zimmerman, p. 357.

[8]C. E. Colton, *The Minister's Mission* (Grand Rapids: Zondervan Publishing House, 1961), p. 178.

8

The Pastor:
Preacher and Teacher

A great pastor must be a preacher and teacher of God's Word. I have never known of a strong church that did not have powerful preaching and teaching of the Word of God.

First Corinthians 1:21 tells us that it pleased God to save them that believed by the foolishness of preaching, not foolish preaching (which is rather prevalent in this day) but by the preaching of the Word.

Jesus set forth the example for preaching. We are told in Matthew 4:17, "Jesus began to preach, and to say, Repent: for the kingdom of heaven is at hand."

Jesus said, "The Spirit of the Lord is upon me, because he hath anointed me to preach the gospel to the poor; he hath sent me to heal the brokenhearted, to preach deliverance to the captives, and recovering of sight to the blind, to set at liberty them that are bruised, to preach the acceptable year of the Lord" (Luke 4:18,19).

Sent To Preach

Jesus sent out His disciples to preach. We are told in Luke 9:1,2, "He called his twelve disciples together, and gave them power and authority over all devils, and to cure diseases. And he sent them to preach the kingdom of God, and to heal the sick."

The Great Commission Jesus gave to His disciples was to "Go ye into all the world, and preach the gospel to every creature" (Mark 16:15). Mark then adds, "After the Lord had spoken unto them, he was received up into heaven, and sat on the right hand of God. And they went forth, and preached every where, the Lord working with them, and confirming the word with signs following" (Mark 16:19,20).

On the Day of Pentecost, moments after the New Testament

church was born, the apostle Peter stood up to preach. The New Testament church was a preaching church: "They ceased not to teach and preach Jesus" (Acts 5:42). "They went every where preaching the word" (Acts 8:4).

The preaching and teaching of the Word of God is primary to the successful church. To build a strong, great, God-honoring church, we must preach and teach the Word. It has a message to proclaim, it has a mission to fulfill.

It is the same message the New Testament preacher was commissioned to proclaim. Luke tells us that the New Testament church born on the Day of Pentecost "continued in the apostles' doctrine" (Acts 2:42), or as most versions say, "they continued the apostles' teaching." This means they continued to teach and preach the Word. They continued in the doctrine Jesus had revealed to them.

Once in a great while, I hear someone say that in his preaching he does not preach doctrine. I am always reminded of the story of the old lady who had a very bad habit of ending almost every sentence with the expression "ner nothin." She heard one preacher deliver a sermon (so-called) and said to him, "I like your preachin'. You don't preach no doctrine, ner nothin."

The Word of God is the doctrine we must believe and teach. We must contend for the faith once delivered to the saints. God said, "I give you good doctrine, forsake ye not my law" (Proverbs 4:2).

The first sermon after Pentecost is of vital importance, for it is a key to the success and power of the New Testament church.

The sermon that Peter preached at Pentecost as recorded in Acts 2 was of about three minutes' duration, but it contained a dozen great doctrines of the Christian faith and resulted in three thousand conversions that day. This certainly ought to prove that a sermon does not have to be everlasting to be of eternal value!

In this first sermon, Peter gave the congregation the kernels of the Christian creed. But it had little grist for the philosophy of the Greeks, the sensuousness of the Epicurians, or the jurisprudence of the Romans. For the Christian, however, it contained about a dozen doctrinal points of the faith.

It is sad to say many sermons of today have no doctrinal content at all. Like the men on Mars Hill, some preachers are very intent on preaching "some new thing."

Some preachers take fascinating mental excursions into vague philosophical areas. Some men love to be ecclesiastical Luther Burbanks: "Marrying a sermonic flower to some new philosophy to produce the odd fruit of a contemporary cultural concept."

It is no wonder a certain man said he joined the church on "confusion of faith." The truths of Christ do not change. Our interpretation of Him might grow, and our means of delivering His message and sharing His truths with the world may change, but God remains forever the same.

When someone exclaimed, "The preacher of today must catch the spirit of the age," another went on to say, "God pity him if he does. Our business is not to catch but, by the eternal truth of God, to correct the spirit of the age."

Too often today the trouble is that instead of the message changing the world, the world has been changing the message.

Too many sermons inspire for the moment, but they do not instruct. Too much of the preaching of this day is wishy-washy. You can listen to sermon after sermon from many pulpits and have real difficulty in finding even a skeleton of a creed.

Simon Peter's sermon at Pentecost was doctrinal. He goes directly to Christology, covering the life and existence of Christ. In this brief message the great apostle preaches the Trinity, identifying Jesus with God the Father and God the Holy Spirit.

He declares the divinity of Christ by saying, "Let all the house of Israel know assuredly, that God hath made that same Jesus, whom ye have crucified, both Lord and Christ" (Acts 2:36).

In verse 23, he preaches about the suffering and crucifixion of Jesus, and in verse 24, he talks about the resurrection when he shouts: "God hath raised [Him] up, having loosed the pains of death: because it was not possible that he should be holden of it."

He also preached about the Ascension when he said: "This Jesus hath God raised up, whereof we are all witnesses. . . . Being by the right hand of God exalted" (vv. 32,33).

In this sermon we also find the doctrine of forgiveness of sins, for when the people cried out, " 'What shall we do?' Then Peter said to them, 'Repent and be baptized every one of you in the name of Jesus Christ for the remission of sins' " (Acts 2:37,38).

Peter also preached to the multitudes at Pentecost about the baptism in the Holy Spirit. He explained to them when they asked, "What meaneth this?" that this was the outpouring of the Holy Spirit prophesied by Joel and declared, "The promise is unto you, and to your children, and to all that are afar off, even as many as the Lord our God shall call" (Acts 2:39).

So in this brief sermon by Simon Peter we have the doctrine of Christ: His divinity, His crucifixion, His resurrection, His ascension, His forgiveness of sins, His fulfillment of His promise to send the Holy Spirit, and His millennial reign. We also have the doctrine of signs, wonders, and miracles; the doctrine of water baptism; the doctrine of faith; and the doctrine of the Holy Spirit.

Inspire and Instruct

A pastor's preaching should be instructive. Preaching must be on a sane, intelligent, instructive basis. We must teach while we plead. The apostle Paul instructed the young preacher Timothy to "rightly divide the word of truth."

The apostle Paul in both of his Epistles to Timothy deals at length with the apostasy that would come in the last days. He said that false teachers would arise, that people with itching ears would not listen to the truth, that they would have a form of godliness but deny the power thereof. He also said that men with corrupt minds, "reprobate concerning the faith," would resist the truth. He added, "Evil men and seducers shall wax worse and worse, deceiving and being deceived."

The apostle then points out, "All scripture is given by inspiration of God, and is profitable for doctrine, for reproof, for correction, for instruction in righteousness: that the man of God may be perfect, thoroughly furnished unto all good works" (2 Timothy 3:16,17).

If any segment of preachers should study the Word, know the truth, be proficient in rightly dividing God's Word, it should be those who are called upon in this present generation to deal with the pagan philosophies of our day.

Successful ministers must discipline themselves to study God's Word and to rightly divide it. The greatest preaching and teaching possible is to be able to dig out of God's Word the great and eternal truths, the nuggets of God's gold, and make them so simple and present them in such a manner that even a child can understand them. Jesus said that we are to "feed His sheep."

Some preaching does not answer the questions of the inquiring heart. It is simply too academic; it is too theoretical; it is so much rhetoric. Sermons should not only be inspirational, but to fulfill God's purpose they must also be instructive and informative.

Sermons should be emotional. The first sermon delivered by Simon Peter at Pentecost was emotional. His hearers were "cut to the heart" (Acts 2:37). Another version says, "They were pricked in their heart." And a third, "Their hearts bled."

It's not enough that people should be mentally stimulated by the sermon, they must be emotionally stabbed by it.

Man is a tripart being: spirit, soul, and body. Salvation affects every phase of his life—his spirit, his soul, his body. His soul is the seat of his affections, his emotions. In order for a person to come in contact with God, he must mentally believe, he must emotionally receive, he must bodily obey. There is no such thing as a true conversion void of some emotion. Being born again affects the mind, the will, and the emotions.

Our faith comes to grips with both the mind and the heart. Evangelism without education will give us fanaticism, and education without evangelism will give us frigidity. We must teach while we plead, and plead while we teach. We must strike for the human heart as well as the human mind.

Peter Marshall once said at Gettysburg Theological Seminary, "The gospel we have to preach is emotional at its highest. That is the message that our people are hungry for in their deepest need. For what could be more emotional than the idea of a suffering God? How could we speak to the Cross without emotion? Calvary is the story of a Man who took things terribly to heart . . . it is the privilege and penalty of the preacher that he must take the gospel terribly to heart, that he must be moved by the things that are happening in our world and in the lives of his people."

The movements of the world are "heart" movements to a great degree. It is still true of our faith that "out of the heart are the issues of life."

Jesus showed emotion in His preaching and teaching while on earth. He became angry at the moneychangers in the temple. With anger, He answered the ecclesiastical leaders; He struck out at hypocrisy with withering denunciation; and when He saw the great multitudes stumbling through life without proper direction, the Scriptures tell us that He was moved with compassion. He wept over Jerusalem.

Move People to Action

The preaching of the pastor should call for action. Peter's sermon moved people to action and called for a decision, "Now when they heard this, they . . . said unto Peter and to the rest of the apostles, . . . brethren, what shall we do?" (Acts 2:37).

That is a thrilling question to follow a sermon. Sometimes we do not drive people to ask it. We do not demand that they do something about it, and so they do nothing.

A well-known preacher had a woman say to him after his sermon, "What did you want me to do tonight?" He said to her, "Did you not know?" She replied, "No, sir, I had no idea." The clergyman was shook to the extent that he went home very upset and spent the night in praying and endeavoring to analyze his preaching. He discovered that his preaching failed to be decisive.

Paul rhetorically asks, "If the bugle gives an indistinct sound, who will get ready for battle?" (1 Corinthians 14:8, RSV). Christian preaching is not only the call to mess, the feeding of the people, but it is also the call to charge, to rise up, march, and serve.

Peter's first audience cried out, "Brethren, what shall we do?" They got a clear, distinct, and definite answer: "Repent." That was the first thing to do. People must come to grips with sin, strike a negative attitude toward it, and repent from the depths of their soul. Then, "Be baptized every one of you in the name of Jesus Christ for the remission of sins" (Acts 2:38).

Next was a promise, "And ye shall receive the gift of the Holy Ghost." This is what they asked for—and this is what they received.

Then followed some instructions on how to live: "Save yourselves from this crooked generation" (v. 40, RSV). Here was a separation from the sins of the world and the ability to live in the world and yet not be of the world.

Then we read, "There were added that day about three thousand souls" (Acts 2:41, RSV). That is constructive evangelism.

It seems almost inconceivable that people, after being converted and hearing the Word, do not join the church.

People need to be taught that the invitation is not only to salvation, it is to service. The Christian does not merely get out of something by following Christ, although we attach much importance to our deliverance from sin and our freedom from guilt. But let it be understood that people also get *into* something. They enlist in the church for service and for the giving of themselves for the work of the Kingdom.

Pastors must teach that the church is the body of Christ and Christ is its Head. We must not separate the Head from the Body. Nobody functions without a head, nor can a head function without a body. In essence, Christ and the church are inseparable, and our preaching, therefore, must lead to the service of the church, as well as to its orders. Converts must not merely be added to the roll, but to some role of service in the work of the church.

Preach Christ

Paul was a successful preacher because he preached Christ. He preached with authority and with power. When he took pen in hand or when he mounted the pulpit, he had authority from God to deliver a message to the people about Jesus Christ. He spoke without apology. He preached with unction and with power.

One of the sad situations prevailing today in the contemporary church is the weak preaching delivered by weak preachers. Today's preaching, in some instances, is clever, analytical, problem-conscious, socially concerned, but it can be all this and be nothing more than an echo of the *New York Times, Washington Post,* or *U.S. News and World Report.*

Paul appeals to preachers to preach Christ, "Christ in you, the hope of glory" (Colossians 1:27). Already in his day apostasy had begun; false theories and philosophies had appeared, void of Christ and void of His reality.

God has not called us to preach our own pet theories, ideologies, or philosophies, but Christ. It is easy to get sidetracked these days. But preach the "unsearchable riches of Christ." There is unlimited material in God's Word that we can preach to the people.

Don't make the mistake of the young cowboy in West Texas who drifted into a meeting in a little town and was gloriously converted. A few days later, he felt the call of God upon his life to preach the gospel. He knew nothing about the Bible, and, in fact, had never read the Bible, so he went into a bookstore to buy one. He was shown a small Bible, whereupon he said to the clerk, "No, no. That Bible isn't big enough. I'm going to be a preacher, and I'll preach that thing up in a week!"

The Bible offers sufficient material to preach a lifetime.

Consider Paul's preaching to the Colossians as a pattern for our preaching. It might be said that his sermon was about a person, a possession, and a prospect. In Colossians 1:28, Paul lifts up the exalted title of Christ when he says, "Whom we preach," not "what we preach."

Christianity includes many things: organizations, institutions, rituals, theologies, traditions—but the gospel is Christ. Preaching is never merely talking about Christ, it is Christ himself being ministered to the people.

The reason Paul's message was about a person was that he had a personal experience and could say, "I know whom I believe." The gospel of Christ is not just an abstract principle, a theory, a philosophy, an ideology, a way of life—the gospel is Christ, a personal, living, dynamic experience of union with Christ through the power of the Holy Spirit.

Paul's message was the message of a person, but it was also the message of a possession: "Christ in you," Christ personally experienced and assuredly known. We must realize that there are many areas of reality in which Jesus Christ is firmly rooted: history, theology, morals, liturgy, the sacraments, ethics—but the emphasis is Christ in *you*—Christ in you, an intimate, dynamic experience.

Paul's message to the Colossians and our message to the world is a message of prospect, a message of hope. It is, "Christ in you, the hope of glory." This looking forward to heaven has been called pie-in-the-sky religion, but "this same Jesus, which is taken up from you to heaven, shall so come in like manner as ye have seen him go" (Acts 1:11). It is one of the major tenets of our faith that Jesus will return in glory.

This prospect has been both a challenge and a comfort. On the one hand, it tells the world to be ready, to be prepared, to be about the Father's business. And those who have accepted the challenge have been sustained through perturbation, privation, persecution. That's why this "hope of glory" has become known as the blessed hope.

The Pastor Is a Teacher

The pastor is given a tremendous mandate when told to "Feed

the flock of God." Not only must he reach men with the message of Christ, but he must teach them about Christ and train them to win others to Christ. We must inspire men to believe God's Word, lead men to choose God's Word, teach men to live for God, instruct men in their service to God. The teaching of believers is indispensable to the cause of fulfilling the eternal mission of the Church.

The apostle Paul said a bishop and servant of the Lord must be "apt to teach" (1 Timothy 3:2 and 2 Timothy 2:24). He also urged Timothy to commit his ministry and doctrines "to faithful men, who shall be able to teach also" (2 Timothy 2:2). Advising Titus, he described a bishop as "holding fast the faithful word as he hath been taught, that he may be able by sound doctrine to both exhort and to convince the gainsayers" (Titus 1:9). Paul also emphasized that those charged with the responsibility of teaching others God's will and way should "speak . . . the things which become sound doctrine" (Titus 2:1).

No function of the church is more important than to teach. Jesus gathered around Him a small group of people whom He called disciples ("learners") and taught them concerning the Kingdom. He sent them out to make learners of others. Is it any wonder that it has been said that teaching was the foundation upon which Christianity became strong enough to conquer the Roman world?

The pastor must impart God's Word by sensible, sound, scriptural, Spirit-anointed teaching. The apostle Paul admonished Timothy, "Strive not about words to no profit, but to the subverting of the hearers" (2 Timothy 2:14). Then in 2 Timothy 2:16, he said, "But shun profane and vain babblings: for they will increase unto more ungodliness."

Right between these two verses that tell us not to strive about words to no profit and to shun profane and vain babblings, he tells us, "Study to show thyself approved unto God, a workman that needeth not to be ashamed, rightly dividing the word of truth" (2 Timothy 2:15).

The implication is very clear: If we do study the Word until we are able to rightly divide it, we will avoid profane and vain babblings and words of no profit; and our preaching and teaching will be with power and authority.

You cannot preach or teach with authority and with power without knowledge. Knowledge is power, knowledge makes for authority.

It is true that our knowledge of the Word must be set on fire by the power of the Holy Spirit. It is also true that we must know what we are talking about to really teach. We cannot teach until we have been taught.

As ministers, we must continuously search for God's truths revealed in His Word. One never graduates from the Bible. We never learn all that the Bible contains. A minister should have a daily time in which he reads God's Word in private or family devotions, but he should also have a daily time for the study of God's Word in order to teach and preach.

The minister who waits until Saturday to prepare his Sunday sermon (or lesson) is remiss. God is just as able to lead you five months before you speak as He is five minutes before you speak.

I found it necessary to plan my sermons months ahead. Sometimes titles for a whole season were announced. I always reserved the right to change for guest speakers or to preach something else if I felt impressed to do so.

In sermon or lesson preparation, I found it profitable to write out the sermon or lesson, or at least to prepare a full set of notes. I did this for at least three reasons: (1) It kept me from repeating quotations, illustrations, and themes too often; (2) it enabled me to confine my lesson or message to a specific amount of time (I learned this from radio and television preaching over a period of many years); and (3) it constituted a permanent form for future use of my messages.

Train People in God's Service

There is a difference in the usage of the word *train and teach* as applied here. To teach is to impart knowledge; to train is to teach how to use that knowledge in God's service.

Many churches fail to grow and fulfill God's purpose and plan because the pastor fails to teach, train, and inspire the members to fulfill the eternal purpose of worship, work, and witness.

Qualified and dedicated workers are an absolute essential to the success of any church. They are basic to the growth of the church. No church will ever be larger, more efficient, or more spiritual than its leaders. For this reason, it is imperative that we train our people to do God's service.

We train by doing. A wise pastor is constantly seeking out personnel from among his congregation that he might teach and train and use in advancing the cause of Christ. He trains by finding work to assign to those who have potential.

The pastor trains by example. The apostle Paul writing to the young preacher Timothy admonished him, "Let no man despise thy youth, but be thou an example of the believers in word, in conversation, in charity, in spirit, in faith, in purity" (1 Timothy 4:12). Then he added in verse 14, "Neglect not the gift that is in thee, which was given thee by prophecy, with the laying on of the hands by the presbytery."

In verses 15 and 16, he admonishes, "Meditate upon these things; give thyself wholly to them; that thy profiting may appear to all. Take heed unto thyself, and unto the doctrine; continue in them; for in doing this thou shalt both save thyself, and them that hear thee."

In the second letter that Paul wrote to young Timothy, he said to him, "The things that thou hast heard of me among many witnesses, the same commit thou to faithful men, who shall be able to teach others also" (2 Timothy 2:2). So the minister, by his example, is to teach the flock to do the work of God in order that they, in turn, might teach others how to do God's work, thus multiplying his effectiveness.

The Pastor as Prophet and Priest

A prophet is one who stands before the people on behalf of God. A priest is one who stands before God on behalf of the people. Prophets are mouthpieces; priests are intercessors. Prophets confront the people with God's Word and the people's sins. The priest holds the people up to God asking for His grace—grace to take away those sins.

It is the prophet's calling to thunder forth both God's law and God's condemnation and judgment upon those who violate that law. It is the priest's responsibility to take to God the sins of the people, reminding both God and the people of the Lord's love, mercy, and grace.

A tremendous statement in John 1:17 says: "For the law was given by Moses, but grace and truth came by Jesus Christ." Truth says, "Thou art. . . ." Grace says, "Thou shalt be. . . ." Truth says, "You are sinful, wretched, miserable, undone." Grace says, "You shall be saved; you shall become a new creature in Christ Jesus. You shall become a member of the family of God, an heir of God, and a joint heir of Jesus Christ."

Truth says, "You have failed; you have sinned again and again; you have tried but you didn't succeed; you promised but you didn't keep your promise." But grace says, "Where you were weak you can be strong and where you failed you can succeed and where you sinned you can be forgiven—'for my grace is sufficient.' "

If the pastor thinks of himself only as a prophet to blast away at the sins of the people and shout forth the judgment of God upon those who violate God's law, he may hurt more people than he helps. But if he thinks of himself as the prophet of God to preach the whole truth of God, and also as the priest of God to bear up to God the sins of the people, he will indeed fulfill the awesome task of a pastor. The writer of Hebrews tells us that Jesus was not a priest "unable to sympathize with our weaknesses but one who in every respect has been tempted as we are" (Hebrews 4:15, RSV).

Dr. Ben Patterson, pastor of Irvine Presbyterian Church, Irvine, California, has said, "A preacher simply does not have the right to blast away at his people with the truth—especially if it is the kind of truth that wounds—unless that preacher is also himself wounded by that truth and heartbroken over the plight of his people."[1]

The pastor must never take advantage of the pulpit to air his pet theories, peeves, and gripes. He should never use the pulpit to preach to one person or a small group in the audience.

Some years ago, a man walked up to me after I had preached in the church in Memphis and accusingly said, "You preached that sermon, that whole sermon, right at me." Whereupon I replied, "No, my brother, I did not preach that sermon just to you. First of all, because I never endeavor to correct one person or a small group of persons from the pulpit when there is something I should say to them in private. Secondly, I did not know that you were guilty of the things I discussed today, and, thirdly, you are not worth a whole sermon where there are hundreds of other people present who need the Word."

Preaching and teaching is more than performing. It is true that the preacher or teacher is center stage, that everything in the service from its very beginning has pointed in the direction of the sermon or lesson. And one's personality most surely is to enter into the discourse. But the purpose of a sermon or a spiritual lesson is not to put on a performance that will draw the applause and appreciation of the audience to the preacher or teacher.

Richard E. Orchard points out, "Preaching has as much variety as there are preachers. Some prefer to stand quietly at the pulpit and speak in a conversational voice. Some use gestures sparingly, while others use them generously. Some enjoy preaching on open platforms where there is liberty to move from one side to another. Still others leave the platform on occasion while delivering their message.

"None of these methods is wrong and none can be called right in itself. The whole personality of the preacher must be involved. All his faculties—body, soul, and spirit—must be engaged in the dynamic act of preaching. Effective speaking involves action, and the entire personality must be involved."[2]

But the performance must never overshadow the message. When the sermon is finished, the people should go from the service saying, "The preacher said so-and-so," rather than "the preacher did this-and-that." It is really not important what the preacher did, but it is of eternal importance what he said! To be a successful preacher one does not have to be a clown, an actor, or a gymnast. I once remarked to a friend of mine who was teasing me about a worn place on the carpet in front of the pulpit in my church, "If you have the dynamics, you don't need the gymnastics."

Preachers should guard against sounding pompous in giving a sermon. Bruce Thielemann wrote, "Preaching is the most public of ministries and, therefore, the most conspicuous in its failure and the most subject to the temptations of hypocrisy."[3] Preaching that has integrity comes from men and women who have wrestled personally with what they are proclaiming publicly.

A. W. Tozer wrote about artificiality: Preachers intoning their sermons with an unnatural voice or speaking with vagueness, avoiding anything that might backfire on them. Genuineness requires that the preacher lay aside superspiritual masks, psuedosuperior roles, and everything that smacks of make-believe. They should, as much as possible, identify with those they address. This is especially true when speaking to a new audience.

Sometimes it is necessary to break the ice by using a story or by telling of an event that links the audience of the locale with the speaker in order to get their undivided attention.

Some years ago I was invited to be one of two speakers for the grand opening (not dedication) of a now famous university. Just when the dean rose to introduce me, an usher handed him a note from the university president requesting that he announce some forthcoming event. The dean had real difficulty reading the announcement and finally said, "I just cannot read the president's writing." There was laughter. He then proceeded to introduce me.

When I arose to speak, I said, "I confess to you I was very nervous and tense waiting to speak in a great university. I am not accustomed to addressing such a distinguished audience. I am more comfortable preaching in a storefront church or a tent or a small rural church, but I discover you have a dean that cannot read and a president that cannot write, now 'them's my kind of people.' " I had the audience's attention for my total address.

Faithful teaching and preaching of God's Word is never in vain. It is not our responsibility to compel people to believe and accept the gospel we preach, but it is our responsibility to preach and teach the eternal Word. God gives the increase. God's Word will not return unto Him void.

This truth was made real to me in such a forceful manner that I shall never forget it. Elvis Presley went through adolescence to young adulthood in First Assembly, Memphis. He moved, along with his parents, to Memphis when he was twelve or thirteen years of age. They attended the services regularly. But he never made a profession of faith or joined the church. And despite what may have been written in newspapers, magazines, and books, he never sang in First Assembly or participated in any of the services other than by attending.

When he became world famous, he was often asked by the media what his religious background was. He would reply, "I attend First Assembly in Memphis." Many wrote that he was a member of First Assembly; others surmised that he learned to sing there!

We received thousands of letters from all over the world. Many of them were very complimentary to the church and pastor for producing such a great entertainer, but many others were extremely critical of the church and the pastor for having such a member. Of course, neither attitude nor opinion was correct.

However, it began to concern me that this young man—who had become the world's highest paid entertainer, who was constantly in the news, who seemed to be very proud of the church he attended—seemed by his actions, preferences, and practices to have no concept of what the pastor had preached and taught all the years he had attended. During that period when I was searching my heart to see if we had been negligent or remiss in our responsibilities as a church, pastor, preacher, and teacher, Elvis Presley (following a Sunday night service) asked to talk to me. An usher took him into my office and came to tell me.

Elvis Presley answered the question that had tormented me for months regarding the faithfulness of the church and pastor to "preach the whole counsel of God." When I walked into my office Elvis said, "Pastor, I am the most miserable young man you have ever seen. I have more money than I will ever be able to spend. I have thousands of fans and hundreds of friends. I have reached the top in the world of entertainment, and yet I am so miserable, so very unhappy, because I am not doing the things you taught me to do and I am doing many things you taught me not to do." That statement told me again that God's Word faithfully proclaimed will not return unto Him void.

For an hour and a half I talked and prayed with Elvis. He confessed his sins and asked God to forgive him. I wish I could tell you that Elvis Presley gave his heart to Jesus Christ that night, but I cannot. He returned to Hollywood two days later to continue his career and his life-style that he said made him the most miserable person in America. My conclusion is that Elvis Presley knew the Word of God, knew the way of salvation, and really wanted Jesus to forgive his sins, to become his Saviour, but he was not willing to accept Him as the Lord of his life.

The pastor does not always accomplish all the things he wants to. He does not always see the spiritual growth and development in the lives of his people that he hopes for. But his calling is not to compel people to do what he tells them—it is his calling to faithfully preach and teach them the Word of God (Isaiah 55:10,11).

NOTES

[1]Ben Patterson, "Five Temptations of the Pulpit," *Leadership* 3 (Fall 1982):107.

[2]Thomas F. Zimmerman, *And He Gave Pastors* (Springfield, MO: Gospel Publishing House, 1979), p. 185.

[3]Patterson, p. 106.

9

The Pastor:
An Administrator

"Administration is the name given to a comprehensive and essential function in any society which carries on through the instrumentality of numerous organizations. It is the function within an organization which is responsible for establishing its objects, purposes, aims or ends, for implementing the necessary organizing and operating steps and for assuring adequate performance toward the desired end."[1]

An organization is a deliberate association of persons who desire to accomplish something together or to realize certain common objectives. The individual members become a part of the large organization because they cannot, by themselves, achieve these objectives as well, if indeed they can achieve them at all. The administrator is charged with the responsibility of directing and facilitating the objectives, purposes, aims, and ends of the organization.

Principles of Administration

Organization Is Absolutely Necessary

The eternal purpose and mission of the church of Jesus Christ is to worship God, minister to believers, and evangelize the world. If one is to fulfill that mission he must plan his efforts and join with others in carrying them out most effectively. Planning, programming, and uniting one's efforts with others is another definition of organization. Good organization is one of the basic factors of a successful church.

God planned and organized in the Creation. The plan of redemption, conceived before the foundation of the world, was a well organized undertaking. That organization is obvious throughout the

131

Old Testament. In speaking of Christ's coming to the world, His death on the cross, His resurrection from the dead, the Bible uses the phrase, "In the fulness of time," again and again. Whose time? God's time—in the fullness of that time which God had planned.

Jesus planned and organized. He said often, "Mine hour hath not yet come" or, "My hour is come." Jesus came into the world according to an eternal and divine plan. He was born in Bethlehem, went to Egypt, lived in Nazareth, rode into Jerusalem, was sold for thirty pieces of silver; He was crucified, buried, and arose on the third day—all in the divine plan of God.

The followers of Jesus organized into groups: The seventy witnesses, the twelve disciples, the three members of the inner circle, the treasurer. When Jesus fed the five thousand with fish and loaves, the Scriptures tell us He had the disciples divide the people into groups of fifty. That is organization.

Our Lord calls a man foolish who would try to build a structure without some real planning and counting of the cost. Or what king, he asks, would fight a war without proper planning? (Luke 14:28-32).

The Holy Spirit planned and organized. He had a very definite time and place to come into the world and to come upon the disciples: "When the day of Pentecost was fully come . . ." (Acts 2:1).

The Holy Spirit set in the Church apostles, prophets, evangelists, pastors, and teachers "for the perfecting of the saints, for the work of the ministry, for the edifying of the body of Christ" (Ephesians 4:12). That is organization. The Holy Spirit placed in the Church diversities of gifts. Paul described them as diversities of gifts, differences of administration, diversities of operation (1 Corinthians 12:4-11). That is organization.

The Early Church planned and organized. One of the first problems to arise in the Early Church came about because of a lack of planning and organization. Some of the people of the New Testament church complained that the widows and orphans were being neglected in the administering of such things as food and clothing (Acts 6). And the church responded with planning and organization.

Administration of the Organization Is Essential

A good administrator sets forth the purposes, aims, and objectives, or ends, of the organization he represents. He must recruit and supervise personnel as provided for in the organization. He delegates and allocates authority and responsibility. Finally, he must oversee the general implementation of the activities he has delegated. Among the chief responsibilities of the administrator then are planning, recruiting, delegating, coordinating, and supervising.

The administrator must provide information, stimulation, and inspiration to accomplish the purpose of the organization. He must be able to evaluate, analyze, plan, and project. He must make provisions for necessary committee meetings, facilities for such meetings, and the coordination of efforts so the group can achieve the purpose for which it came into being.

The Pastor as an Administrator

"It is impossible to separate the work of ministry from that of administration. Linguistically the two words are cognate and for the Christian pastor they are inseparable. Administration concerns the total care of the church and may be thought of as including 'ministry.' "[2]

Inasmuch as administration concerns the total care of the church, the success of the pastor and the church will largely be measured by the pastor's success as an administrator.

"The word for pastor in the New Testament is *poimen*. It means a shepherd, one who tends herds or flocks (Ephesians 4:11). Pastors guide as well as feed the flock. This ministry of shepherding was committed to the elders who were also overseers (Acts 20:17,28). Paul says to the elders of the church in Ephesus, 'Take heed therefore unto yourselves, and to all the flock over which the Holy Ghost has made you overseers' (v. 28)."[3]

The three terms of *elder, bishop,* and *pastor* are brought together in Acts 20:17,28. We can, therefore, conclude that the pastor is an elder or overseer. His work requires tender care and watchful superintendence. The Greek word for "overseer" in the New Testament is *episcopos*. It is usually translated "bishop," but the literal meaning is "overseer." The ultimate responsibility of the organization, supervision, inspiration, and success of a church must largely be accepted by the pastor. Doubtless many pastors have failed in their total task simply because of their lack of administrative ability.

The pastor must be the administrator of all the work of the church.

Good organization and procedure would make him an *ex officio* member of all committees, boards, and groups in the church. Of course, he is the shepherd of the flock and must not, in his administrative responsibilities, forget his spiritual obligations to those with whom he labors.

Coordination of Departments, Facilities, and Programs

The pastor should be the most knowledgeable person in the church regarding every facet of its ministry and program. He should be able (for it is his responsibility) to communicate to all individuals, committees, boards, and the total congregation the purposes and priorities of the church, as well as the responsibilities of all individuals and groups within the church.

Organizations, groups, and even athletic teams must work together to succeed, accomplish, or win. Without good leadership, few organizations succeed and few athletic teams win. In many cases friction, a lack of cooperation, and failure are caused by a lack of communication, coordination, and effective leadership.

Craig Thomas, a little boy who had gone to school only two days, announced to his grandmother, "That teacher and I are going to have trouble." His grandmother, surprised, inquired, "Why, Craig, what do you mean, 'have trouble'?" The youngster replied, "Well, I can't read and the teacher won't let me talk." The problem was poor communication, and even the child recognized where it would lead.

The overlapping of responsibilities and authority of the various departments and personnel can be avoided by a strong administrator who has the total church ministry in focus and is able to coordinate plans, efforts, and facilities.

The coordination of the use of church facilities and equipment is very important to a church whose varied ministry necessitates the multiple use of its facilities and equipment. Some churches, by careful coordination, are able to use the same facilities for Sunday school, youth meetings, senior citizens activities, men's ministries, women's ministries, and recreation, as well as a day school. The church with many activities of a varied nature will have conflicts and confusion over meeting dates and inadequately prepared facilities unless a coordinator—the pastor or someone he designates—provides direction, assistance, and firm leadership.

A church calendar is absolutely necessary. Every meeting to be held during the year (including date, time, room, and anticipated attendance) should be listed on the calendar. A good administrator will see that one group or department does not infringe on the prerogatives of another group. For example, the men's group should not be allowed to plan its meeting on the night that is scheduled as choir rehearsal night, and the day school should not schedule a basketball game in the gym on the night a revival meeting is in progress in the sanctuary.

Efficient Direction and Involvement of Personnel

Too often a pastor finds himself doing menial tasks and attending to matters in the church simply because he has failed to plan his work and organize his congregation. His time is taken up "majoring in minors," rather than doing the primary work God has called him to do.

The first seven deacons were appointed so the apostles could give themselves to prayer and to the studying and preaching of the Word (Acts 6). It should be noted that the pastors of the New Testament Church provided for the selection of these men to administer the ordinary, nevertheless important, affairs.

One of the tragedies of the ministry in this day is the lack of time the pastor has to devote to prayer, to studying the Word, and to feeding the flock over which God has made him overseer. The average pastor's time is taken up with so many minor tasks and secondary matters that he has little time for the primary responsibility. Woodrow Wilson often spoke about men who were "defeated by the secondary."

A good pastor is one who understands his priorities—what is major and what is minor, what is primary and what is secondary. He then organizes his time, his efforts, and his congregation in a manner that will give him time to pursue the major tasks. This can be done successfully only when the pastor is a good administrator and is able to assign to others the secondary tasks.

Placing Spiritual Matters First

The pastor is the chief human administrator in the spiritual work of the church. The use of the term *administration* in relation to the spiritual emphasis and environment of a church may seem at first to be a conflict of ideas, but it is not. Although God himself initiates the spiritual life of any group of Christians, He uses the pastor to lead the congregation into deeper spiritual experiences and to direct the efforts of the church in fulfilling the Great Commission.

So the pastor is the God-ordained administrator of the spiritual program of the local church. He administers the ordinances of the church: water baptism and the Lord's Supper. He conducts the rites of the church: weddings, funerals, dedications, installations, and other functions that are important in the life and ministry of the congregation. The ordinances should be administered in such a manner that they will teach the lessons Jesus intended. The various ceremonies can be conducted in such a manner that they will become instruments in fulfilling the mission of the church.

For example, in administering the Lord's Supper, the pastor should emphasize its scriptural basis as well as its significance to the believer. This ordinance is called the Lord's Supper because it was instituted by Jesus at the Last Supper (Luke 22:19,20). The term *Eucharist* is also used. While not used in the English Bible, it is based on a Biblical concept. It is taken from the Greek word *eucharistia*, which means, "The Thanksgiving." We also refer to this service as Communion (1 Corinthians 10:16). The Greek word translated *Communion* really means "fellowship." There are other names given to this ordinance of the church: *The Sacrament, The Breaking of Bread, The Lord's Table*. However, the meaning of this ordinance of the church is to commemorate the death of Jesus and to anticipate His return. It is a time of giving thanks to God for the supreme price He paid through Christ, and it is a glorious time of fellowship with Jesus and our fellow believers.

The pastor must be prepared physically, mentally, and spiritually. Charles Erdman says that the Communion service must be "conducted with dignity, solemnity, and the feeling of tender emotion. Yet there must be a spirit of confidence, cheerfulness, and hope."[4]

Every detail of this service should be carefully planned. The pastor, as well as the men who assist him in administering the ordinance, should be dressed in conservative and appropriate attire.

Water baptism is an ordinance of the church and should be administered by the pastor to all who have believed in Jesus Christ and have accepted Him as the Lord of their lives. Water baptism is an outward sign that an inward work of grace has been wrought. The wise pastor will stress in his pulpit ministry, his personal counseling, and his teaching situations the scriptural position regarding this act of obedience. Provisions should be made to baptize all who believe as quickly as possible.

Water baptism is the rite of entrance into the Christian church and symbolizes the spiritual life begun. The Lord's Supper is the rite of Communion and signifies spiritual life continued. Water baptism is administered only once, for there can be only one beginning of the spiritual life. Communion is administered frequently, teaching that spiritual life must be nourished.

The pastor must give proper emphasis to these ordinances of the church. The nonliturgic approach to Christianity may cause us to neglect these important elements in our witness and worship. Once we understand the significance of water baptism and the Lord's Supper, then we must teach our people in observing them.

Weddings, funerals, dedications, installations, and other functions are very important in the life of the minister and his congregation. These ceremonies can be conducted in such a manner that they will become instruments of fulfilling the mission of the church.

Funerals afford an opportunity for the pastor to be of genuine service to a family bereft of a loved one, and often to get acquainted with members of the family he has not yet met. The funeral provides an opportunity for the pastor to calmly project the real issues of life, death, and eternity.

Of the hundreds of funerals I have participated in, the funeral making the greatest impression on me was in an Episcopal church. When a prominent Memphis attorney, who was charismatic, went to be with the Lord, I was asked to share in the funeral. Upon opening the service the rector, also charismatic, simply said, "We are gathered here today to celebrate the homegoing of Brother George Harsh," and turned the service to me for prayer and my remarks. In that service every song, every utterance, every musical note, was victory—a true celebration! The whole service was what I have long felt should be the type of funeral service for the faithful follower of Jesus Christ.

The dedication of babies provides a wonderful opportunity to explain the responsibility of parents in bringing up their children.

Dedication of their baby is more than just a form through which they go, but they, in fact, are agreeing to bring the child up in the fear and the admonition of God.

The dedication of buildings or other things having to do with the work of the church should have great significance. In Memphis, year after year, on the first Sunday of April, we rededicated our church facilities and ourselves to the Lord. The people repeated the same declaration of dedication they made at the original dedication of the building. It had a very solemn effect on the people, resulting in many recommitments of lives, time, and treasures to the work of God. Such an annual observance served to remind the people of the true purpose for which the facilities had been erected.

The installation of church officers (deacons, Sunday school teachers, or others) provides an opportunity for the pastor to give great emphasis to the responsibilities and privileges of leadership in the church of Christ. Just as an example: After reading a passage from *The New English Bible* in Acts 6:3,4 and in 1 Corinthians 3:8-14, we had the deacons who were to be installed stand before the altar. We said to them: "(name of deacon), if you here and now agree to these requirements for your life and conduct, and pledge by God's help and grace to so live during your term as a member of the church board of First Assembly of God, if you reaffirm your commitment to God and your pledge to this congregation to fulfill your responsibilities with fidelity, courage, faith, humility, and love, please kneel before the altar to have the anointing oil (a type of the Holy Spirit) poured upon you, and to have the hands of the brethren (a type of authority and power) laid upon you in the presence of God and this company of believers."

The minister is expected to administer the worship, work, and witness of the church. This includes the worship services. He should lead or direct the spiritual services in such a manner that there is a spiritual warmth and the meetings are Bible-centered, Christ-honoring, and Spirit-filled.

Worship services, evangelistic meetings, Bible studies, and committee or board sessions should be well planned in every detail and properly announced. All participants should be confirmed, all facilities must be prepared, all equipment should be checked and in working order. In the work of God nothing should be left to chance.

All meetings should begin exactly at the announced time. It is wrong to keep people waiting for a meeting, beginning fifteen or twenty minutes late. Most intelligent and busy people will not attend such meetings often. In this organized world, we must move with the clock. Services should be planned in the most minute detail, yet left flexible so that if in the planning one has missed God's plan, the program can be changed to accommodate His will for that particular service.

Much depends on the minister's own spiritual condition, his attitudes, his responses, his hunger for God, and his desire to lead the people in genuine worship, intensive study of the Word, and successful service.

Assuring a Strong Fiscal Program

The pastor is responsible for the financial welfare of the church and the administration of its fiscal program. He is also responsible for teaching his people both the obligation and the reward of faithfulness in supporting God's work through tithes and offerings. God's plan for the financial support of His work on earth was and is the tithe and offerings of the people. (See chapter 10 where we deal with the pastor and church finance.)

The pastor must be responsible for the overall management of all employees of the church, including the pastoral staff and all other employees: clerks, bookkeepers, secretaries, nursery workers, janitors, maintenance people, kitchen employees, etc.

A church operational manual should clearly set forth job descriptions; employee benefits; use of church properties and equipment; financial policies and procedures (e.g., in making gifts, wills, and bequests); responsibilities of church standing committees, boards, and individuals appointed to offices; and policies regarding weddings, receptions, funerals, rehearsals, recitals, etc., held on church property. There should also be workday schedules, such as hours, lunch periods, days off, sick leave, absentee reporting, payday, termination of service (by resignation, release, or dismissal); all compensation and benefits, such as hospitalization, pensions, holidays, vacations, and emergency leave.

Of course, all schedules, working conditions, compensation benefits, etc., must be set by each church and be compatible with what it wants and needs. Again, I point out that the size of the church and the number of paid employees will determine the portfolio assigned to various persons. Here are two examples for a fairly large church:

Business Administrator

Supervise all buildings, equipment, grounds

Direct all maintenance and custodial personnel

Manage office personnel, food service personnel, and food services

Supervise all buses, including maintenance, use, schedules, and drivers

Maintain schedule of all buildings for all events except regular services

Be responsible for issuing and controlling keys to all buildings

Purchase all building and office equipment, supplies, materials, and insurance

Direct preparation of budget and work with budget committee in subscribing the annual budget

Advise on budget expenditures

Direct local benevolence

Serve as liaison with church and parking lot ushers

Schedule all printing

Perform any other duties requested by the senior pastor

The business administrator shall be responsible only to the senior pastor and shall be at the senior pastor's disposal at all times. He shall keep the senior pastor informed of all phases of the work for which the business administrator is responsible.

Financial Secretary-Bookkeeper

Keep books for the church

Make up and issue checks for payroll and keep payroll files

Prepare monthly and annual financial reports

Prepare monthy and annual line report on budget expenditures

Perform any other work necessary to keep a clear and accurate set of books

Keep payroll files for Christian school

Prepare all F.I.C.A. and withholding forms

Prepare and mail out all W-2 forms for church employees and school employees

Assist with budget preparation and campaign

Keep records of all individual gifts to church on Kardex (visible record) file

Mail out quarterly receipts for all offerings recorded on Kardex

Mail receipts immediately for all offerings received through the mail

Count, prepare, and deposit all money received by the church

Assist in any other work that needs to be done in the office

Good administration will direct and supervise the proper use of all church property and equipment. A couple of pages from First Assembly's operational manual headed "Use of Church Properties" sets forth the following:

A. General Policies
   1. All buildings and properties owned by First Assembly of God, Memphis, have been dedicated to God for worship, preaching, teaching, evangelism, character building, and related activities that honor Jesus Christ and serve the community.
   2. Regular scheduled meetings and services shall have prior claim to space, facilities, and equipment.
B. Administration
   1. Before scheduling an activity requiring a meeting room or other space assignment, a request for such space shall be made in writing to the Business Administrator's office so that all assignments may be coordinated and recorded on the church calendar of activities.
   2. It is particularly important that the scheduling of weddings, rehearsals, ceremonies, and receptions be done well in advance in cooperation with the Business Administrator. Use of recreational facilities shall be scheduled through the Recreation Director's office.
C. Direction on use of the buildings
   1. The policy of the church shall be to use the total facilities to the best advantage in carrying out the purpose of the body.
   2. The use of decorations, the changing of furniture, attaching of materials to walls, and items of a similar nature shall be done only with the advice and consent of the Business Administrator.

3. The organ and pianos are under the care and supervision of the Minister of Music and may not be used without his consent.

4. The sound systems are carefully designed. No additions or changes in the facilities shall be made without the express approval of the Business Administrator in conjunction with the Minister of Music.

5. No temporary structure will be built anywhere on the premises without the consent and supervision of the Business Administrator. The limitation refers to such items as platforms, structures, or devices that attach to the floor, wall, or ceiling, or that may damage coverings.

6. Use of any portion of the property shall conform to the fire and safety ordinances.

7. The custodians and personnel of the church shall move all equipment and furniture when it is necessary and shall see that it is in the proper place for regular meetings.

8. Food and beverages may be consumed only in the following areas of the buildings: nursery area of the educational building, vending machine area, snack area, the dining room of Hamill Hall, and the dining area of the high school building.

9. Use of the kitchen and its equipment may not be made except with prior arrangement by the church hostess and Business Administrator.

10. No flash pictures shall be made during any regular scheduled service in the sanctuary except when specific permission is granted by the senior pastor.

11. Smoking is not permitted in any building at any time.

12. Church facilities may be used for the following:

    (a) Baby showers (for first child only—It is suggested that showers for any succeeding baby be held in some home or other facility in order to help relieve the crowded schedule for use of church facilities).

    (b) For the same reason as listed above it is suggested that church facilities be used for 25th and 50th wedding anniversary receptions only and other wedding anniversary receptions be held in some home or other facility.

    (c) Bridal showers may be held at the church when either the bride or groom are members of First Assembly.

(d) When the dining room and/or kitchen is used for one of the above, such use must be cleared with the church Business Administrator and church hostess.

(e) When showers or receptions are scheduled on a Saturday or Sunday, a small custodial fee is required.

D. Equipment

1. Projectors, recorders, and other visual equipment of the church shall be loaned for outside use only with the approval of the director of Christian Education and First Assembly Christian School Principal, and then *only* when properly checked out in writing. Permission for internal use shall be arranged through the Director of Christian Education.

2. Approval of the recreation director is required before recreation equipment is used or loaned.

3. Lending of equipment other than visual aid and recreational is to be done only through the office of the Business Administrator. A written record of loaned equipment must be provided. In any event, lost or damaged equipment shall be replaced or repaired by borrower. Lending equipment shall be discouraged.

E. Food Service

1. Reservations: All regular weekly and monthly dinner meetings have priority on dining rooms. All other groups using kitchen and dining rooms must clear dates and use with the church Business Administrator. Meal reservations must be made according to policy.

2. Lending and selling: The church hostess is responsible for written records of the lending of all dishes, supplies, equipment, and for receipts from the local sale of food or supplies. The lending of church-owned equipment shall be discouraged.

3. Accounting: The Business Administrator is responsible for collecting and reporting all food funds. The church hostess is responsible for purchasing kitchen items and in preparing monthly inventory of food and supplies.

4. Sanitation: The church hostess shall see that the preparation of food and food facilities comply with regulations of the board of health.

F. Guidelines for use of dining room

1. Requests must be made in writing on forms provided.
2. Approval will be given by letter or phone.

Of course the average church would not need such an elaborate plan for its equipment and facilities, but each church should provide for the proper use and protection of its facilities and equipment. Regulations, therefore, can be written according to the need.

Perhaps one of the most widely criticized policies of the church today is its practice of raising and distributing funds. The church financial policies and procedures should be so administered as to render sincere criticism void. The financial policy of the church should be known to the total membership.

The church books should be open to any and all members of the congregation. The church leadership should do everything possible to keep the congregation informed of the financial dealings of the church. An intelligent and informed congregation is more likely to support the church's financial program than the congregation that does not know the financial policies and procedures, where the money comes from, who spends it, and what it is spent for.

First Assembly/Memphis Manual on Financial Policies and Procedures states:

The church board through the senior pastor shall have the responsibility of administering the financial policies and procedures of the church as outlined below:

1. The Church Treasurer shall be responsible for all money, insurance policies, and valuable papers. He shall be responsible for the preparation of the monthly financial statement.
2. Checks drawn against any account of First Assembly of God Church shall be countersigned. Any two of the following names must be manually signed on each check: Senior Pastor, Church Treasurer, Church Secretary, or Church Business Administrator.
3. Handling of money: Under the direction of the Church Treasurer, only deacons and other authorized personnel shall handle all money. The money will be counted, bagged, sealed by authorized personnel, and taken immediately and deposited in the bank's night depository. All money received during the week is to be counted, recorded, and a receipt furnished by the financial

secretary to staff members and others. Careful attention is to be given to the proper recording of each individual's gifts to the budgetand to all designated causes.

4. Purchases of supplies, equipment, and services that are to be charged to the credit of First Assembly shall be made only on the authority of a purchase order which has been approved by the Business Administrator or Senior Pastor. The purchase shall be authorized only if there is sufficient money credited to the appropriate budget item or items against which said purchases shall be charged. In the event there is not sufficient funds credited in the appropriate budget item or items, or if the supplies, equipment, or services are not budgeted items, prior approval of the purchase must be made by the church board and/or the Senior Pastor.

5. Money collected by the Sunday school, Men's Fellowship, WMCA's, WMC's, Omega-Alpha Fellowship, or any other church organization shall be submitted to the Church Treasurer and properly accounted for through the church books and records. No special offerings may be taken for any event (for example, showers, anniversaries, benevolences) in the Sunday school without the express consent of the Director of Christian Education and the Senior Pastor. Approval should be circulated in advance in writing to the departmental superintendent or class teachers. No special offerings may be taken in any church department meeting (for example, choir, women's and men's groups, youth meetings) without prior approval of the Senior Pastor.

6. The signatures of the Church Treasurer and Senior Pastor shall be sufficient evidence of authority to transfer, convey, or to sign stocks and/or securities in the name of the church so long as said signatures are certified by the church Secretary.

The annual audit shall be made of all books and accounts of the church by a firm of Certified Public Accountants approved by the church board.

Although such an extensive policy and procedure in handling church finances may not be applicable to all churches, each church should formulate and publish a policy and procedures statement. It is the responsibility of the pastor, as the overall administrator, to see that the church of Jesus Christ never comes into disrepute because of the way it handles the money that God's people have contributed toward the advancement of the cause of Christ.

The Pastor and Personnel

The pastor is responsible to recruit, select, train, organize, appoint, and direct church personnel, both paid and volunteer workers.

No church is likely to ever be larger or stronger than the vision of the pastor and those with whom he surrounds himself to carry out the ministry of the church.

The pastor should organize church workers in order to avoid duplication, to be certain that no area of ministry is neglected, and to see that all workers who desire to serve are used in some capacity.

The church I pastored in Memphis is organized in a manner that involves scores of members in various facets of ministry. The church has twelve members on its board of deacons. Each board member chairs one of twelve lay committees. These are operational committees appointed by the senior pastor to assist and advise in expediting the work and ministry of the church. These committees are responsible to the pastor. They have no legislative power or authority to establish policy; they simply serve in an advisory capacity to the pastor and the official board of the church. Seldom does a person serve on more than one committee in order to provide a place for more members to serve.

The duties and responsibilities of the committees are carefully outlined. Each committee member, when appointed, is provided with a list of his or her duties and responsibilities. For example, the finance committee and the maintenance committee are charged with the following specific responsibilities:

Duties of the Finance Committee

1. Review the general finances of the church and make recommendations as to the means and methods of increasing revenue.
2. Review the proposed budget each year and make recommendations to the official board.
3. Recommend ways of economizing wherever possible.
4. Make recommendations for the purchasing of supplies, and the undertaking of needed maintenance.

5. Review salaries of staff and employees and make recommendations in keeping with the findings.
6. Give full support to the annual budget campaign.
7. Work with the various departments of the church in raising funds and keeping departments on a sound financial basis.
8. Work with the pastor on all fund-raising campaigns.
9. Provide an audit of the books annually.
10. Make reports to the official board from time to time.

Duties of the Maintenance Committee

1. Give attention to the upkeep of all buildings, equipment, and grounds.
2. Make recommendations regarding repairs, remodeling, and maintenance of buildings and grounds.
3. Regularly inspect church buildings, parsonage, equipment, and grounds to determine needs of same.
4. Advise or recommend the purchasing and securing of materials and equipment that will provide the best economic and satisfactory results in keeping with our buildings and equipment.

If a church operates a retirement home, nursing home, or a day school on the premises, careful and prayerful administration is required. Many times the same facilities are used for church functions as well as a day school. The church and school often must share classrooms, assembly halls, gymnasium, kitchen and dining hall, etc. This requires careful and considerate scheduling to avoid conflicts. When many of the enrolled students and occasionally some of the teachers are not members of the church, it is essential that all policies and procedures are set forth and administered fairly.

First Assembly, Memphis, operates a Christian day school, kindergarten through grade 12, having an enrollment as high as 733. Its manual sets forth guidelines for its operation. First Assembly Christian School operates as a ministry of First Assembly of God. The senior pastor of First Assembly appoints the First Assembly Christian School board. The membership of the board consists of twelve members of the church along with the school principal serving as an ex officio member.

The First Assembly Christian School board operates the school under the general guidelines determined by the senior pastor and the church board. The principal serves as the board's agent in carrying forth policy and daily operation of the program.

It is the principal's responsibility to make regular reports to the board on such matters as personnel, finances, spirituality. It is the belief of First Assembly Christian School that only an education of this type will firmly establish Christians for times like these.

An example in careful administration is seen in the following item from the church manual: "The gym is scheduled by the Recreation Director for both the church and First Assembly Christian School. Basically the school uses the gym until 5:00 each afternoon. Scheduling is done for the church after 5:00 P.M.. All games and practice times are to be scheduled by the Recreation Director for the school and the church.

"Scheduling for school games is done in advance and is coordinated with the church activities. When school activities are performed in the gym, the responsibility for supervision of these activities is left up to the principal of the school and the team coaches in connection with the Recreation Director.

"The keys to the gym are given only to the Recreation Director. But only the Business Administrator is authorized to give or loan a gym key."

The pastor should be responsible for the employing of all professional personnel and should have general oversight of the appointment of all volunteer workers.

I am convinced that one of my strengths as a pastor of the same church for thirty-seven years was in the fact that I had the final word on all those who were employed by the church, from cook to assistant pastor.

I also had veto power over any person (except deacons) who filled any office or position in the church, including ushers, bus drivers, and coaches. The pastor was always consulted before anybody was asked to serve in the church. When the pastor has the power to select all personnel, he has the power to control the church program.

One of the responsibilities of a good administrator is to provide ample information and to publish regulations governing various events likely to occur on church premises using church facilities, such as weddings. Weddings, at times, are highly emotional events. There is much room for misunderstandings and sometimes ill will. Therefore, very clear policies should be published and distributed to those who request the use of church facilities for weddings. An example: "The bride shall clear every detail with the church receptionist. The persons involved should make an early appointment with the officiating minister. After he has agreed to perform the ceremony, the secretary will then fill out a church wedding record form stipulating date, time, facilities, and service desired. Then an appointment shall be arranged for the bride with the minister of music and with the church hostess if the wedding reception is to be held at the church. Because of the difficulties in securing adequate help, no wedding rehearsals or weddings may be scheduled on the following days: New Years Day, Independence Day, Labor Day, Thanksgiving, or Christmas Day. No wedding shall be scheduled to begin later than 8:00 P.M. "

Premarital counseling is absolutely necessary. Premarital counseling should be provided by the church (at no extra charge), covering ideals of the Christian home and the personal commitment in the marriage vows. Premarital counseling should be scheduled at the earliest convenience (at least six weeks prior to the wedding date if possible).

The minister of music must be consulted about the choice of music for weddings and receptions. Some music played and sung at weddings is not acceptable in all churches. The choice of the organist and the vocalist should be left to the discretion of the bride, but all music must be approved by the minister of music.

Since the sanctuary is already furnished as a place of dignity, it should not be elaborately decorated. Be certain that wedding decorations do not damage floors, rugs, walls, or furniture. Nails and screws must not be driven into any part of the building or furnishings. Such adhesive materials as adhesive tape are not to be attached to painted surfaces. Carpets must be protected from damage caused by dripping candles. The florist engaged by the bride should be responsible for all decorating, and required to remove all decorations from the church building immediately following the wedding ceremony. The florist is responsible for any damage caused by decorations.

When the wedding party arrives at the church for the rehearsal, the bride or her mother should be prepared to provide the following information in order that the rehearsal can proceed without delay:

Who will direct the rehearsal (other than the minister), who will light the candles, who will seat the mothers and other persons to be seated as part of the service, how many family pews will be reserved, who will be the head usher, and a list of attendants.

Because the wedding ceremony is a sacred occasion, flash photographs are not to be taken by anyone during the ceremony. Other photos, such as time exposure, may be made at any time. When a reception is to follow, the photographer is to be instructed by the bride or her parents that everything possible should be done to expedite the taking of pictures after the ceremony in order not to delay the reception afterwards or unnecessarily consume the time of participants or guests.

All wedding receptions at the church should be held in the dining room, if possible. The church hostess may serve as caterer for the reception if the bride desires. If an outside caterer is engaged, the caterer must clear all arrangements in advance with the church hostess, who is responsible for the use of the facilities.

Some miscellaneous rules will often prevent embarrassing situations, such as smoking is not permitted anywhere in the buildings, no alcoholic beverages will be served on the church premises at any time, no wedding or rehearsal will be conducted when any member of the wedding party is under the influence of alcohol, no rice or confetti may be thrown anywhere in the church building.

Some churches may wish to establish fees for the organist, vocalist, and the minister. There is no charge made by most churches for the use of buildings and facilities. Other churches find it necessary to charge a small custodial fee, which includes opening and closing the buildings, checking the temperature, rearranging the furniture before and after the ceremony, and clean-up following the wedding and rehearsal.

NOTES

[1]Ordway Tead, *The Art of Administration* (New York: McGraw-Hill Book Company, 1951).

[2]Ralph G. Turnbull, ed., *Baker's Dictionary of Practical Theology* (Grand Rapids: Baker Book House, 1967), p. 314.

[3]Ibid., p. 318.

[4]Charles Erdman, *The Work of the Pastor* (Philadelphia: Westminster Press).

10

The Pastor and Church Finance

God's plan for the financial support of His church on earth was and is the tithes and offerings of His people. Pastors and church leaders should not be embarrassed or hesitate for one moment to speak often and freely about man's stewardship and his obligation to God.

The Bible is clear and emphatic in its teaching regarding man and his money. God's Word emphasizes God's ownership and man's stewardship, especially in the teachings of the Old Testament. Jesus spoke often and forcefully concerning man and his money. The majority of His sayings deal with property and the right use of property. One out of every sixty verses in the four Gospels deals with stewardship. Money is spoken of in the Bible six times more than water baptism, forty-five times more than the Lord's Supper.

The pastor in most churches is responsible for the financial programs. He at least must provide leadership in this area. Therefore, the church financial program should be scriptural, spiritual, and sound—and thus successful.

The patriarchs, prophets, and priests taught and practiced tithing. Jesus and the Early Church taught and practiced tithing. I believe that Bible-believing Christians today will teach and practice tithing.

The church's financial program should be a spiritual program. God's program for financing His work on earth is a strengthening, character developing program. It teaches the ownership of God and the stewardship of man.

In church financing we must keep constantly before our people the spiritual aspect of stewardship. If our people are consecrated to God and their lives are Spirit-filled, financing the church program should be no problem.

Tithing is not a financial matter, but a spiritual one. Spiritual people have no difficulty giving to God that which belongs to Him. When there are "frictions" regarding our giving to God it is because there are "fractions" in our consecration.

Methods of raising money for the Lord's work should be sanctified, sensible, and scriptural. Some of the methods used to enhance God's work and His church must cause the angels in heaven to blush and the Son of God to turn away in shame.

Contrast this type of service with a Biblical type of giving in 1 Chronicles 29:9. There we are told that when the Children of Israel brought their offerings before the Lord, then the people rejoiced over what had been offered so willingly, and David, the king, also rejoiced with great joy.

Financial matters of the church should be conducted in a precise, sound, and business-like manner. Complete records of receipts, expenditures, and individual donors should be kept. There should and must be regular reports to the board, to the church, and to the individual members.

The financing of the church can be successful when it is scriptural and sound and mixed with faith that you are operating in the will of God, and that God is concerned about the financial needs of the church.

Many churches have discovered that the better way to operate their financial program and to assure meeting their obligations is to operate on a strict budget, and to get the congregation to pledge, or underwrite, that budget in advance.

What Is a Church Budget?

The church budget reflects a church's commitment to carry out the Great Commission (Matthew 28:19,20 and Acts 1:8). Few ministries are performed by a church that do not require money. Thus, the church budget becomes a list of ministries to be accomplished during the year for which the budget is planned.

The ministries included in the church budget express what the church understands its purpose to be. This means that a church budget involves more than a list of items with a dollar amount allotted for each. A budget includes plans and provisions for reaching specific goals.

Church budgeting is an expression of Biblical faith and should be based on a theology of stewardship. A church with a commitment to mission ministries, evangelism, and the growth of Christian members will do a thorough job in planning all phases of the budget.

There are four general divisions in a church budget:

1. Ministries
2. Service to and support of those ministries
3. Church plant, grounds, and equipment
4. Debt retirement, insurance, and contingency.

Through the use of a budget, the church income is divided properly among the things the church would finance. The divisions of funds are a matter of great importance. God's money should be managed in such a way as to bring honor to Him, and to show the seriousness with which we care for His business.

More specific division, of course, would depend upon the church—its ministries and the divisions that would expedite the handling of funds for that particular church. First Assembly, Memphis, had a line budget with thirteen identified lines: 000—Administration, 100—Promotion and Public Relations, 200—Maintenance, 300—Sunday School, 400—Athletic Activities, 450—Youth Division, 500—Children's Division, 600—Music Department, 700—Adult Ministries, 800—World Ministries, 900—Debt Retirement, Interest, and Insurance, 1000—Contingency, 1200—New Equipment and Capital Improvements.

For a church and its leadership to successfully control the contributions and expenditures of a church budget, it must be a unified budget. Each department of the church should be assigned an expenditure budget and operate its department within that budget.

Here is an example taken from the bylaws of one church.

Article 4—Finance, Section 1—The Budget (A) The church shall operate on a unified budget. (B) Each department of the church shall be assigned an expenditure budget and shall operate its department within said budget. (C) All monies received in any or all departments for budgetary purposes shall be deposited with the Church Treasurer for the unified budget. (D) All monies received by any or all departments for any purpose shall be properly accounted for and deposited with the Church Treasurer.

To secure funds for capital expenditures, such as a new building, additional land, an expensive organ, equipment or furnishings, several means may be used.

Some churches launch a campaign to raise, in cash, a certain amount for a specific project: some endeavoring to raise the total cost of the project; others having a goal of one-fourth or one-half of the total.

Many fund-raising programs are for one, three, or five years. This is a very good method, but a very difficult one.

A conventional loan is a simple means of securing the money needed. However, sometimes it is impossible for a church to borrow the money it needs at that time. (A conventional loan is one made by a bank, savings and loan association, an insurance company, or some other financial institution to which the church pays interest and mortgages its property.)

Many churches have found that the issuing of bonds is a viable means of financing church buildings. There are two kinds of church bonds: mortgage bonds where the church mortgages its property to the bondholders; and debenture bonds, actually a note the church gives to the bondholder. Both the mortgage and the debenture bonds bear interest.

There are bonding companies that will prepare, issue, and sell the bonds for the church for a fee. This is often a rather high fee. At times, using such a company would be to the church's advantage. However, a church can issue and sell its own bonds. (This can be done with the same type of organization, with minor modifications, used to raise a pledged budget.)

In issuing church bonds, a reasonable interest should be paid for several reasons. It will assist in selling the bonds in a reasonable time. It will allow some who feel they cannot donate the money to invest it instead.

In most cases, much of the bond issue will be sold to members or those with some connection to the church. These folks like to feel that their money is being used for God's glory while it provides some income for them.

Another point in favor of bonds to finance capital expenditures is that when raising the budget, you are taking pledges to pay the interest and maturities of these bonds—for the most part held by these same people.

It is possible to use a combination of cash drive and bond sale, but one should never confuse selling or buying bonds with a donation. The church should never speak of the bond as a donation, nor should the church suggest that the individual buyer might want to donate the bond to the church.

Many will, at the time the bond matures, donate it to the church, but that should not be suggested by the church in order to assure a good sale of the bonds. It should be considered strictly a business transaction.

The church sales emphasis should include the money's potential in the hands of the church, the offer of a fair rate of interest, the use of one's money to advance God's program, and the soundness of the investment.

One can use a combination of a conventional loan and a bond sale if debenture bonds are used. In 1960, when First Assembly, Memphis, planned to build its new sanctuary and other facilities on North Highland, the church could not secure a sufficiently large loan; it was necessary to issue $300,000 in debenture bonds and to borrow the balance through a conventional loan.

Many churches have found that the Church Builders Plan operated by the Stewardship Department of the Assemblies of God is a good way to finance the purchase of property and the erection of buildings.

Why the Church Needs a Budget

The church needs a budget to maintain its financial integrity. A budget will enable the church to pay its obligations when due. Church bills ought to be paid on time! We must not be guilty of the attitude that a church is not compelled to meet its obligations. We must not bring discredit and dishonor to the cause of Christ by handling church finances carelessly and irresponsibly.

A budget provides facilities for worship, for teaching and training, and for evangelism. The budget sees that sufficient funds are available to teach, train, develop, mature, and establish every member of the church, as well as to minister to the shut-in, sick, the hospitalized, the discouraged, the distressed, the lonely, and those with problems of any kind.

These various needs of the families of our churches should not be left to happenstance; with a budget properly distributed, each area of need can be met.

The budget provides for local outreach, for church services, for the musical program, for visiting preachers, teachers, and evangelists, for visiting musical groups, for choirs and soloists who are paid an honorarium out of the budget. Local evangelism and benevolence of the church should be written into the budget.

Radio and television are very important means of reaching the masses. The budget can provide these ministries without appealing to the radio-TV audience for funds. This ministry can be written into the church budget.

The church should provide for world ministries in the budget to enable participation in national and worldwide missions.

Through the use of a budget, the church income is divided properly among the things the church would finance rather than to have it receive an offering for each item, perhaps receiving more than enough money for some things and not enough for others.

Sufficient time should be allowed for preparing and compiling the church budget—at least three months. The budget is exceedingly important to every phase of the church's ministry and operation. Therefore, no part of the church's work should be overlooked in the budget. It is necessary that those charged with the responsibility of preparing, compiling, and adopting the budget go over every detail in order that nothing is left out. Otherwise, you will find yourself calling for one too many special offerings to cover what was overlooked.

Compiling the Budget

To compile the budget, each department, for example, youth, Sunday school, missions, should determine its needs for the year, then compile the total. Prepare a budget worksheet showing the budget divisions, amount of the budget for each department last year, the amount spent, and the third column will show the proposed budget for the new year.

The head of each department should prepare a list of things the department will need funds for in the budget year.

If the department has a department committee, the budget for the department should be gone over with its committee.

The department budget then should be submitted to the senior pastor and business administrator for their approval. It is absolutely necessary that all department budgets be submitted to the senior pastor for his approval.

In most larger churches, the business administrator compiles the complete budget submitted by all the departments, after which the budget goes to the finance committee for review. After the finance committee has studied the proposed budget, line upon line, and made whatever revisions it has, it recommends the final proposed budget for adoption. (It must be adopted by whatever group the church constitution/bylaws authorizes, the board or the church membership.)

Publicizing the Budget

The amount of the budget should be announced to the congregation, pointing out how the budget dollar is spent. It is absolutely essential that the congregation know what the budget figure is, what the budget includes, why so many dollars are necessary for each department and each project.

The leadership of the church should use this occasion to mention the various ministries of the church and how very important each is to fulfilling the eternal purpose.

If the church publishes a paper or a weekly bulletin, there should be a series of stories, beginning when the budget is adopted, about the church's commitment to certain missionaries, mortgage or bond holders, etc. Other matters one could well discuss would be maintenance, utilities, equipment, and, of course, the value of youth, children, senior citizens, singles, and what it costs to maintain these departments.

If a church paper or bulletin is not available, the pastor and other leaders should take just three or four minutes in every service for weeks until everybody is well acquainted with the budget. Emphasize one facet of the budget each service. The church should use every method at its disposal to publicize the budget and inform the congregation.

The Scriptural Basis for Giving to the Budget

Giving begins in our hearts. Paul commended the Macedonian

church for its generosity and liberality and added, very significantly, "The Macedonians gave first themselves."

Our giving is manifested in dollars, time, talent, energy, service, devotion, and worship. Money is a means of exchange. It represents brawn, brains, sweat, and toil. To give money is to give a part of ourselves. To withhold our money is to withhold a part of ourselves. We cannot possibly give ourselves to the Lord without giving our money also.

Why are we to give? It is an obligation. God is the owner of this world and all that there is in it, and man is God's steward: "The earth is the Lord's, and the fullness thereof" (Psalm 24:1); "The silver is mine, and the gold is mine, saith the Lord of hosts" (Haggai 2:8).

By virtue of His creation and providence, this is God's world. Ultimate ownership is with Him. Long centuries ago the Psalmist said, "The sea is his, and he made it: and his hands formed the dry land" (Psalm 95:5). The property which we hold is subject to the prior rights of the Creator and of the Owner.

We are totally dependent upon God for all things. They belong to Him by the indisputable right of creation, and man should recognize God's ownership. He is living on God's property, using God's money, breathing God's air, living in God's world, dependent upon God for everything that he has, spiritually and materially.

The tithe is an acknowledgement of God's ownership and our stewardship. The tithe is not just a bit of ancient legalism; it is a confession of faith wrought in deeds rather than in words. More than paying a debt, tithing is a form of worship. It is a practice that relates divine truth to one's daily living, for man is obligated to give God at least a tithe of his income.

More than an obligation, tithing is a glorious and happy privilege: In so doing one shares in the great work of redemption. This is a ministry in which not even the angels in heaven can participate.

How are we to give? Let's follow the Scripture's rules for giving. First, according to income. In Deuteronomy 16:17, we are given the Old Testament rule for giving to God: "Every man shall give as he is able, according to the blessing of the Lord thy God which he hath given thee." The apostle Paul carries the same principle into the New Testament when he says, "Upon the first day of the week let every one of you lay by him in store, as God hath prospered him" (1 Corinthians 16:2).

Ezra says that the Children of Israel "gave after their ability unto the treasure of the work" (Ezra 2:69). Luke says, "Then the disciples, every man according to his ability, determined to send relief unto the brethren which dwelt in Judea" (Acts 11:29).

The apostle Paul sums up the rule of giving when he says, "If there be first a willing mind, it is accepted according to that a man hath, and not according to that he hath not" (2 Corinthians 8:12).

The Holy Scriptures further establish the fact that *tithing* is the basis of our giving, that one tenth of our income belongs to God. "All the tithe of the land, whether of the seed of the land, or the fruit of the tree, is the Lord's: it is holy unto the Lord" (Leviticus 27:30). In Malachi 3:10, God instructs the Children of Israel, "Bring ye all the tithes into the storehouse."

If the Bible teaches anything about our responsibility to the Lord and His work, it teaches tithing. It teaches that ten percent of our income is the basis of our giving to God. Actually, until we have tithed, we do not give God anything. Giving begins after tithing.

We are to give regularly, "Upon the first day of the week let every one of you lay by him in store, as God hath prospered him" (1 Corinthians 16:2). We are told in Proverbs 3:9, "Honor the Lord with thy substance, and with the firstfruits of thine increase."

The only way to enter into a successful partnership with God is to regularly and faithfully give to the work of God—not just sporadically or when we are emotionally moved.

We are to give cheerfully, "Every man according as he purposeth in his heart, so let him give; not grudgingly, or of necessity: for God loveth a cheerful giver" (2 Corinthians 9:7). Our giving to God is a cheerful and delightful experience when we have earmarked and laid aside the tithe of our income as God has commanded.

And the Bible is just as clear on *where* to give as it is on how to give. Malachai 3:10 says, "Bring ye all the tithes into the storehouse." The storehouse in Israel's day was the depository for funds to carry on the work of God. Out of the storehouse, the priest, the singers, the porters, and the workers of the tabernacle were paid and the various expenses attached thereto were met.

We are told in the New Testament that the people brought their offerings and gifts and laid them at the apostles' feet, which, of course, means that they brought their offerings into a center. From this treasury, distribution was made for the carrying on of the New Testament Church.

Underwriting the Church Budget

Any size church can and should operate on a budget. Any size church can underwrite and pledge its budget. Why?

1. It makes possible the projection and plans for growth and development.

2. It assures the availability of funds for planned projects.

3. It commits the people to the support of their church first.

4. It stimulates an increase in giving.

Credit cards prove that most people will spend more using a credit card than if they have to pay cash. Many people, if they are pledging to the budget of the church, will pledge more and pay it than they would contribute if they gave cash week-by-week during the year.

In 1959 before First Assembly, Memphis, began to operate on a pledged budget, the church collected a total of $142,000. In 1960, the church went on a pledged budget; in 1983 it collected in all funds $2,300,000.

Marvin Gorman, pastor of First Assembly of God in New Orleans, says that the offerings in his church increased by 50 percent the first year he was on a pledged budget, 36 percent the second year, and has continued to show an increase each year.

5. It reveals fiscal responsibility on the part of the church.

In 1947, when the Memphis church decided to relocate and erect a new building, we could borrow only about 30 percent of the money we needed for the project. When it became necessary again to move and build new facilities, we could not secure a conventional loan for the $850,000 we needed. We had to sell $300,000 in debenture bonds to supplement the amount we could borrow, the cash we had on hand, and the money from the old church property.

By using a pledged budget and other responsible fiscal operations, the church had established sufficient confidence that in 1970, in one day, it sold $400,000 to individuals in debenture bonds, and in 1974, in one day, $750,000 in bonds. In 1978, the church announced it would sell $246,000 in bonds on October 1. Before the bonds were printed, the total issue was sold out. That is an excellent example of the confidence that a church builds when it is fiscally responsible.

6. It becomes a witness of the people's concern for Christ and His church.

7. It makes numerous financial drives and pressures unnecessary.

First Assembly, Memphis, has assets of perhaps $6,000,000. The church bought its present site; built its sanctuary, educational building, activities building, high school building; bought three additional acres; spent over $100,000 remodeling the educational building for school, multiplied thousands for school and church furnishings and equipment; and established a school—yet there was never a drive to raise funds for these projects, nor has there been a building fund drive since installing the pledged budget system of financing.

8. It teaches giving to Christ through the church rather than on one's own, giving to whatever program or project that might strike one's fancy.

Pledging

We all pledge for other things, why not God's work? We make pledges almost daily: some for time, some for our life, some for eternity.

We pledge to (or promise) the Lord that we will live for Him when we are saved, we pledge when we marry, we pledge when we join a civic group, we pledge when we buy our home, we pledge when we buy insurance, we pledge when we take a job or hire an employee, we pledge when the utility turns on our electricity and gas. Our lives are filled with promises to make good on some commitment. Is there really any legitimate reason we should not pledge a portion of our income to God and His church?

There are many questions about pledging the budget that a church member may ask. Why pledge? How shall I make my pledge? How much should my pledge be?

When one signs a pledge card, it is simply an estimate of what one expects to give, based on one's anticipated earnings.

To pledge to tithe one's income to the church is to back the church's future. One's signature will influence others to do likewise. Signing will help a person to overcome the tendency to indifference. It does not create or increase his obligation to give—whether he ever signs a pledge card or not, he is obligated under God to tithe his income—but formally making a pledge does accentuate his obligation.

Signing will help to keep him from unnecessary expenditures. It will help him to put God's money where it belongs; it will assist him in putting God first.

Signing is doing one of the most effective things to make powerful the testimony of Jesus Christ in the pulpit, in the denomination, and on the mission field. It is a business-like way of doing the Lord's work. It denotes one's loyalty to his church, a church Christ left to carry on His work.

At least ten things will determine how much, and how enthusiastically, a person pledges: His Christian faith, his interest in the church program, his recognition of the need of his church, his concern for the church's future, his financial ability, his willingness to sacrifice, his desire to encourage others to sacrifice, his willingness to trust God, his faithfulness in prayer, his belief in the commands and promises of God regarding tithing and sacrificial giving.

Most churches make pledges or commitments in order to operate. They could not have much ministry without making commitments. For example, the church makes commitments to missionaries; bondholders, or mortgage holders; pastors and other employees; utility companies; supply houses; advertisers; printers; programs; evangelists; guest speakers; singers; various departments and projects of our denomination, including aged ministers, national and district home missions, national and district women's and men's ministries, national orphanages, and Bible colleges.

Now a logical question is, If we expect our church to make such commitments, then why shouldn't we be expected to commit a portion of our income to the church to pay for these things?

Every individual who worships at the church should be expected to make a commitment toward the church budget. It is so necessary for everyone to do his or her part, whether large or small. It is essential that the leadership of the church feel and know that everybody who worships is on the team doing what he or she can do.

With everyone doing his part, the church budget can be subscribed and underwritten in a very short period of time. God demands only that we do our part.

Every person who worships at the church should be asked to

pledge a tithe or at least to make a definite commitment of some amount. Persons who fail for some reason to turn in a pledge within a given time should be contacted by a budget team member and asked to make a pledge. We should never antagonize those who do not pledge, but we need to assure them that we are anxious that they, too, "get on the team." All who worship at the church should share in its obligations as well as its blessings.

What does the church pledge include? The pledge should include one's tithe, missionary offerings, offerings in evangelistic campaigns, Sunday school, in fact, any money a person plans to give for any cause through the church.

Before making a pledge, however, there are things one should do.

1. Look to God in gratitude for His abundant blessings and gracious goodness.

2. Recall what the Bible says about stewardship.

3. Consider the scope of the work of the church, asking God for a vision of the needs at home and abroad.

4. Ask the Lord to guide in making the pledge.

5. Discuss the matter with family. It should be a family project. There may be times when various members of the family who have income of their own would want to make a separate pledge.

6. Ask for faith to give sacrificially.

If one will do this, the church budget will be pledged and the work of God will move forward.

The leadership of the church might do well to tell the people that they will not be sent reminders of their progress in paying their pledges. The Memphis church told the people that their pledge to the budget was a sincere commitment to *God*, but in the event their financial status changed (a loss of a job, a decline in business) their pledge could be reduced or cancelled with no questions asked.

In twenty-five years First Assembly, Memphis, always collected more in the budget fund than was pledged! Most pledges were always paid. If somebody failed to meet his pledge, it seemed others were always blessed beyond what they expected and gave more than they pledged. And, too, new people coming into the church after the budget was pledged made contributions.

Some years as much as $70,000 above the pledged budget was given in the budget fund. I always believed that it was the special blessings of God upon a people who were trying to do all they could to fulfill the eternal purpose of the church.

Those who do not wish to pledge toward the budget should not be antagonized. If you do not make the matter an issue, you will perhaps get the money they would have pledged anyway. Some of those who appeared to be so stubborn in the beginning became exceedingly enthusiastic in their support of a pledged budget.

We should not take frequent offerings for items not budgeted. Projects during the year not covered by the budget should be held to a minimum. If we ask the people to pledge for the budget and come back again and again for offerings for items not in the budget, the next year people will commit only a portion of their tithes and offerings to the budget and hold some for other offerings. This, in effect, defeats our purpose for a budget.

Organizing the Budget Campaign

The pastor should appoint a budget campaign chairman. If desirable, the pastor could have the church board approve his appointment or have the church board select a chairman. Personally, I preferred to select the person and ask the board to approve.

The budget campaign chairman should be a person of sterling character, a person in whom the congregation has utmost confidence, a person with influence in the church. He or she will be the key to the success of underwriting the church budget.

The chairman must be a faithful and enthusiastic financial supporter of the church. Otherwise he will not be able to convince the members of the congregation that they should pledge to the budget.

He should be able to speak in public, presenting the budget forcefully, succinctly, sincerely, and convincingly.

If the chairman is one who can solicit other workers and command their respect, enthusiasm, and effort, the campaign is likely to succeed.

The pastor and chairman should select a vice-chairman. The vice-chairman should be a man or woman with as many of the aforementioned qualities as possible. Something might occur that would make it necessary for him or her to assume the chairmanship. In any event, the vice-chairman will play an important part in the budget campaign.

The pastor, chairman, and vice-chairman should appoint division chairmen. If the church is large enough to require it, the membership should be divided into divisions in order to adequately reach everybody. There can be two, three, four, or more divisions if needed. Under these division chairmen will be group leaders. These may be appointed according to the need.

A steering committee is very important to the budget campaign. This committee should consist of the pastor, the budget campaign chairman, and the vice-chairman. The division chairmen may also serve on this committee. Others may be added, for example, the associate pastor, the business administrator, and the church treasurer.

The organization and number of personnel can be tailored to meet the size of the congregation.

Various responsibilities are assigned by the steering committee. The success of the campaign depends on the careful assignment, and the faithful carrying out, of those responsibilities. The steering committee should meet at least three months before the actual campaign is launched to appoint the group leaders and team captains, to decide on the theme for the budget campaign (a good theme is very important in a successful campaign), and to select a date to launch the campaign.

The day that the campaign is kicked-off is usually called Commitment Day. It is essential to the success of the campaign. We will deal with Commitment Day later, but at this point I want to emphasize that the date should be selected weeks in advance, the date publicized and promoted in every way possible.

In setting Commitment Day, great care should be taken that it does not fall on a long weekend holiday, such as Labor Day, Fourth of July, or Memorial Day. It should be a day that will provide the best opportunity for the most people possible to be present. I like to emphasize that it is a day when we commit to God our all: our lives, our families, our time, our talents, and our treasures.

To launch the campaign, some churches have a budget banquet for the congregation. Others have a worker's banquet only. The logistics of a membership-wide campaign is rather difficult and expensive. If the church provides a complimentary budget banquet, it can run into the thousands of dollars (depending of course on the size of the congregation and the type of menu served). If each member of the congregation is requested to buy a ticket, some may not be able to afford the luxury and others may not want to spend their money to hear a "pitch" for a subscribed budget.

I always had a banquet for the campaign personnel rather than for all the church because I liked to have the initial pledging on Sunday morning in a worship service.

Usually the workers banquet was held on the Friday or Saturday night before Commitment Sunday. Such a banquet could be held at any time convenient for the congregation.

Information is dispensed at the banquet: Again the amount of the budget, the divisions of the budget, the need for the budget, etc., is emphasized. Copies of the budget brochure, copies of the responsibilities of various workers, copies of the budget itself, are given to the workers.

Inspiration is also provided. Information and instructions are vital, but will not accomplish nearly so much as when those receiving the information and instructions are inspired to carry out the direction.

A multi-media presentation of the various ministries of the church and how the budget enables the church to implement these ministries is always an inspiration. Skits are sometimes used to dramatize the work of the church and the vital place the budget plays in that work.

Usually the pastor or someone he chooses gives a brief message on why the church should have a budget, what the budget will enable the church to do next year, what ministries the church supports, why everybody who worships at the church should support the budget.

Responsibilities

Chairman

The chairman is responsible for the overall campaign and its total thrust. This, of course, is under the pastor and all decisions are subject to the pastor's approval.

The chairman is responsible to provide speakers for various church functions, before and during the budget campaign. Weeks before the budget campaign actually opens, there should be someone in all groups (such as men's ministries, women's ministries, youth, children, and Sunday school) who would be responsible to keep constantly before the people that the budget is soon to be pledged and that it is important to pray that God will direct in the campaign.

About a week or two before Commitment Day, the chairman should select persons who are able to forcefully and succinctly (in about four or five minutes) discuss the forthcoming budget in Sunday school classes and departments, and especially in the Sunday morning and Sunday night services the week before Commitment Sunday. The same procedure should follow on Commitment Sunday and until the budget is totally committed.

Division Chairmen

In addition to serving on the steering committee, the division chairmen should supervise the group leaders. The chain of command is that the team captains report to the group leaders, who report to the division chairmen, who in turn report to the budget chairman.

Group Leaders

A list of responsibilities for the group leaders are prepared and put into their hands soon after they accept the position in the campaign. These are the responsibilities:

1. Attend the budget campaign leadership banquet.

2. Lead the way in making your own personal pledge in the Sunday morning commitment service.

3. Pray for God's help and guidance in coordinating the activities of the teams under your supervision.

4. See that every person on your team is personally contacted and given an opportunity to pledge to the budget.

5. Meet your team captain on a specified date to give him the list of persons he is to contact.

6. Meet with your team captains to receive and compile the reports.

7. Encourage your team captains by telephone or in person to followup on Monday and Tuesday nights any who were not reahed Sunday or had not fully made up their minds regarding their pledges.

8. Keep in close touch with your team captains until all on their list have been contacted and the captains are in position to complete their report.

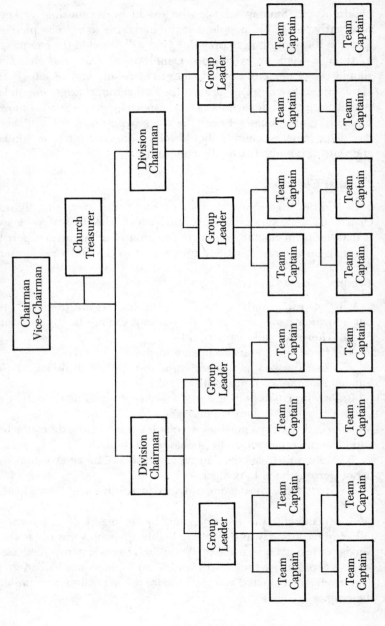

BUDGET CAMPAIGN ORGANIZATION CHART

9. Meet on a date specified by the steering committee with your team captains to receive the final report of your team captains. It is imperative that you have this complete report from each team captain.

10. Keep in close touch with the chairman of your division.

11. Be enthusiastic in encouraging your team wherever possible.

Team Captains

The team captains are those who do the actual follow-up in the budget campaign. The second Sunday after Commitment Day, following the Sunday service, they contact all those who have not made a pledge toward the budget. They may telephone or visit those on their list. If people are not at home or yet undecided, they may be recontacted Monday or Tuesday night of that week.

The diagram on the opposite page is an organizational chart. You see the number of people involved and the positions they fill. Again, I point out that you need people to contact only your congregation, so the size of the membership would determine the number of teams you need.

Responsibilities

1. Lead the way in making your own pledge on Commitment Day.

2. Pray for every person to pledge.

3. Ask the Lord to direct you in your approach when you call on the people.

4. Two Sundays after Commitment Sunday meet following the morning service.

5. Call on or telephone that afternoon all who have not pledged. Note your results.

6. Make report to group captain that Sunday evening.

7. Monday and Tuesday, phone those who weren't home on Sunday.

8. Report regularly to your group leader.

9. Meet group leader the next Wednesday evening.

10. Don't let up for a moment. Your task isn't finished until all have been personally contacted.

Some person or persons should be assigned for every facet of the campaign (such as publicity, promotion, brochures, signs, printing of pledge cards and envelopes). Many letters will be sent during a successful campaign: letters to all who are requested to work in any way in the campaign, and a letter of thanks along with a list of responsibilities to those who accept.

Letters should be sent to all workers, reminding them of the workers banquet and Commitment Day and how important it is for them to attend both. These letters are usually signed by the chairman or the pastor, or both.

The board should send a letter to every member of the church the week the campaign opens, telling them what the budget means to the church and its future, expressing the hope that everybody will pledge, that everybody will get on the team.

One of the beautiful results of a successful campaign is not only the money that is raised for the work and ministry of the church to fulfill its eternal purpose, but to have scores of the people of God working together in a beautiful spirit of cooperation to accomplish the work of God.

Commitment Sunday

Commitment Day can become one of the greatest days in the church calendar. It is a day that people make a commitment to God of their money, jobs, families, and, most importantly, their lives. It's more than a pledge of money; it becomes a commitment of life, time, talent, and treasure. The pastor speaks that Sunday on commitment, challenging the people to make a total commitment to the Lord. At the close of his message, he invites the people to come forward with their families and present their commitment at the altar where the pastor has special prayer for them, for their homes, for their children, and for their businesses or jobs.

The week before Commitment Day, the pastor and church board should have written to every family, enclosing a pledge card and envelope, telling them again how much the budget is, how important it is to underwrite the total budget, how the church depends on each person to do his or her part, large or small. The family is asked to pray about the matter, to discuss it, to bring the pledge with them to church on Sunday, and to be prepared as a family to bring the pledge down to the altar when asked to do so by the pastor.

It is indeed an inspiring sight to see hundreds of families come forward to make a definite commitment to God of life, family, and finance.

Follow-Up

On Commitment Day not only are pledges taken in the morning service, but in the evening service as well. Usually about 80 percent of the total budget is subscribed Sunday morning. The amount is reported Sunday night, and again pledges are received. On that Sunday, between 80 and 90 percent of the total budget is usually received.

During all services that week the people are given an opportunity to make a commitment. A report on the progress of the campaign is given in every service, not only verbally but by various visible means, such as overheads, blackboards, and signs.

In securing church pledges, confidentiality is essential. Many people are very disinclined to let other people know what they contribute to the church. Therefore, along with the faith promise card, there should be an envelope in which the pledge may be enclosed. The people should be told that only authorized persons open the envelopes.

Follow-Up Reports

The team captains are together on the second Sunday of the campaign to receive their assignments of those who have not pledged. They report to their group leaders on that Sunday evening, giving a detailed account of the contacts. They keep the names of those they were unable to talk with and try again on Monday or Tuesday. They then make their final report on Wednesday night.

In every service during the campaign, there should be a report on the progress in pledging the budget and a call for the balance. When the budget is completely subscribed, then there should be a victory report of the job well done!

Budget Controls

The handling of money should be directly supervised by the church treasurer, the deacons, or other authorized personnel. The counting of the offering should be done by the tellers. Two or more persons should always be present when handling or counting money. Some type of form should be used for showing the amount and on which the two persons counting money can attest the amount with their signatures.

All money received from tithes, offerings, and any other sources should be accounted for by the church treasurer. All monies received by the church treasurer should be deposited by him in a bank designated by the church board. The money should be deposited the first banking day after it is received. Large sums of money should be counted and carried to the bank immediately for an after hours deposit. The church should carry insurance that will cover any loss, inside or outside the church premises.

All monies collected by organizations in the church (for example, Royal Rangers, Missionettes, Men's Ministries) should be properly accounted for through church books and records and accounted for by the church treasurer.

Audit

The official board of the church or the finance committee or some person or persons authorized to do so should provide an audit of all the books annually by a professional public accounting firm, preferably a CPA.

It is vital that a church endeavoring to borrow money, issue bonds, or make any financial transaction of any consequence should have an annual audit and statement of assets and liabilities. Such an audit must, of necessity, be made by professionals.

Purchases

A purchase order system and/or check request should be used. A purchase order should be approved only if it is an authorized budget item and sufficient money is available. All invoices/check requests should be checked and verified by department heads before approval of payment is made.

Goods should be received or services performed before any payment is authorized. If a church has tax-exempt status, check to see if the invoice includes sales tax and if a discount is given if paid within a certain time limit.

Good management control within a church should require that all checks be countersigned. Each check should reflect the budget line item the check is to be drawn against, along with a brief description of what the payment is for.

Reports

Monthly financial reports and budget line balances should be prepared and furnished to the pastor, the church board, and other persons who have a need to know.

An annual report of the audit should be distributed to the church membership in the annual meeting of the church congregation.

The church books should be open to all members of the congregation. The church leadership should do everything possible to keep the congregation informed of the financial dealings of the church. An intelligent and informed congregation is more likely to support the church's financial program than an ill-informed one.

The financial program of the church is vital to its success. The pastor's leadership in this area is essential. Just as the pastor endeavors to lead his people in worship, in Christian service, and in witnessing, he must teach and lead his congregation to be faithful in giving of their material substance to assure sufficient funds to fulfill the eternal purpose of the church of Jesus Christ.

11

The Pastor and Church Growth

God planned for His church to grow. God intended that the church of Jesus Christ be aggressive, always on the offensive, not just holding the fort.

It is quite interesting to observe that wherever a mighty spiritual move is recorded in the history of the New Testament church, a report of great church growth usually follows.

Genuine church growth (that is, where people turn away from their sins and accept Christ as their Saviour and Lord) is impossible without spiritual power. On the other hand, it is impossible for the church to have spiritual power and not grow.

In church matters, spiritual power means growth—growth spiritually, numerically, financially, and in ministry and influence.

Certain factors and spiritual elements cause church growth: personnel, organization, follow-up, facilities, promotion, hard work, and spirituality. The spiritual elements in church growth as recorded in Acts 4:23-31 are prayer, the power of the Holy Spirit, the spreading of God's Word, witnessing, great grace upon the church members, and the giving of money and being united in effort.

Personnel

Next to spirituality, perhaps the most important factor in the ministry of the church is the personnel. The qualifications and commitment of the personnel, both professional and volunteer, will determine what the church becomes.

Qualified and dedicated workers are essential to the success of any church. They are basic to the growth of the church. No church will ever be larger, more efficient, or more spiritual than its leaders. Finding qualified personnel is one of the great problems in churches today—not just paid personnel, but volunteers who are consecrated, Spirit-filled, and trained to do the work that needs to be accomplished.

I believe that many churches fail to grow and fulfill God's purpose and plan because the pastor fails to teach, train, and inspire the members to fulfill the eternal purpose of worship, work, and witness.

The pastor is responsible to recruit, train, organize, involve, and direct both volunteer and paid church workers. Most churches need many nonpaid workers for the scores of ministries that must be covered.

Recruiting volunteer workers in these exceedingly busy days is not an easy task. One of the chief complaints of industry and business today is their inability to recruit employees who are energetic, loyal, reliable, enthusiastic, and intelligent. Unfortunately, the same shortage of dedicated workers exists in many churches.

There are several ways a pastor can recruit volunteer workers for the various ministries of the church. First, he should give personal attention to the individual believer. A good administrator of the church will study the individual members in his congregation.

He will constantly be on the lookout for those who have talent, those who can be trained and used in God's work, and those whose commitment is such that they are willing to be involved in the work of the church. He will personally solicit them for the Lord's service.

Second, the pastor should emphasize the spiritual privileges, opportunities, and responsibilities as he enlists workers. They should be taught that whatever service is rendered, it is as unto the Lord and, therefore, should be done well.

I recall a well-known radio personality who became involved with a charismatic group and received the Holy Spirit. He joined our church. He later said that he came to the church excited about this newfound experience and expected to hear a great deal of preaching about the joys, the victories, the glories of the baptism in the Holy Spirit. Instead, for the first six months, he heard sermon after sermon on stewardship: the stewardship of time, of talent, and of treasure. He added that he discovered there was much more to Christianity than just singing and shouting about the fullness of the Holy Spirit; he discovered an accounting to God for our stewardship in the service of God.

Third, the pastor can survey the membership periodically. A card or form should be provided for the people to fill out, indicating the kind of service they would like to render to the Lord through their church. New members should also be asked to indicate the service they prefer to render. This type of survey should be made annually.

Christian education is indispensable to the ministering church. The church should use Bible studies, Bible classes, Sunday school, Christian day school—every means available—to teach and train people for places of ministry. The Great Commission demands that the church minister to the believer through the teaching of God's Word so he is grounded in the eternal Word of God and conformed to the image of Christ.

If the church fails, it will fail because it lacks dedicated, committed members who are willing to give themselves energetically and freely to the work of God. Many business enterprises fail, not because of no market for their product or inability to produce the product at a profit, but because of inefficient personnel. If businessmen have real problems with the personnel they hire, and if they find it difficult to secure efficient, faithful, energetic, and enthusiastic workers for pay, how much more difficult it is to enlist faithful, energetic, efficient, enthusiastic workers for the church who will donate time and energy without financial compensation.

All this points up that the pastor, as an administrator, must be active in recruiting, training, and involving the members of his church in fulfilling the church's mission in today's world.

Organization

Simply put, good organization in a church is the delegating of responsibilities, and requiring accountability for those responsibilities. Good organization means everybody with a job and everybody knowing what that job is. We can go so much further and get there so much faster by organizing and planning our efforts.

In 1958, Gene Martin and I were on a preaching mission in East Africa. One day we went with two missionaries into the bush to photograph lions. We were in a specially built pickup truck. We pulled off the trail among a pride of lions and were able to get rather close to them. We had been told that the lions were not likely to attack us unless they were hungry. Of course, we had no way of knowing whether or not they were hungry!

When we had taken all the pictures we wanted and were ready

to leave, we discovered to our chagrin that the truck was stuck in the sand. The driver said, "You will have to get out and push," whereupon I replied, "Wait a minute! Let's get organized. Let's all get out at the same time, and all push together at the same time, then when this truck comes out of the sand, it's every man for himself!" That's organization out of necessity.

But good organization plans ahead, providing a church calendar on which special events, special days, and certain goals are set.

Goals help lift our sights, reach our potential, enlist the cooperation and the enthusiasm of our membership, and assist us in making each member feel that he counts. Goals give direction. Without goals, we often do not know where we are going and where we are when we get there. Various goals can be set: goals in visitation, recruitment, attendance, finance, and many other areas. There should always be something for which to strive—an aim, a goal.

Good organization means setting up various departments in the church, such as Sunday school, youth, children, senior adults, men's and women's ministries. It also includes assigning workers and facilities to these departments and providing them sufficient funds in the budget in order to minister to all segments of the church.

Organizing a corps of ushers and training them to serve in an important place in the church is a vital factor for church growth. Berry Terry, church administrator at First Assembly in Memphis, says, "Ushers can make a definite spiritual contribution to the church. We cannot exaggerate the importance of good ushers. . . . When the usher takes seriously his job, prepares for it, and is found faithful, he renders an inestimable service to his church and his Lord."

Proper organization provides for complete records in every department of the church: records of membership, finance, attendance, visitation, shut-ins, hospitalized members, absentees, etc.

In churches where I pastored, we always kept records. For example, in the Sunday school we kept records on the pupil, the absentee, the prospect, the visitor, the teacher and officer, and the total school. I found good records invaluable in the operation of a church.

Some people do not like to keep records because they don't like details. Others dislike records because it's like looking into a mirror. For some of us, it's rather discouraging! Records *are* a mirror. Records reflect what we do or fail to do.

I recall teaching a men's Bible class of around two hundred fifty, for which detailed records were kept. I recall how astonished an attorney was who had occasionally visited the class. One day I talked to him on the phone and mentioned that our records showed he had been in attendance so many times in the past year. I mentioned some of the exact dates. He was so impressed with the efficiency of the operation of the Sunday school class that he began to come regularly—and later became a member of the church.

Think of the records kept of baseball players, football players, basketball players, and others. Consider the records kept on a business transaction. Is not the work of God more important than athletics or business? Records should be kept and records should be used by the pastor who is interested in church growth.

Promotions and Publicity

An important factor in church growth is promotion and publicity. It is essential that various programs and services the church offers be conveyed to the general public. The ministry of the church needs to be promoted within the church and publicized in the community. The first ingredient in promotion is information. The pastor must see that his congregation is fully aware of scheduled events.

E. S. Caldwell asked the question, "Why is 'high visibility' so important? Take a look at the churches with impressive growth rates and you will discover every one of them is highly visible within its community. Not every one has an ideal location but, despite that fact, the existence of each is known to the general public."[1]

It is essential today that the church get the attention of the public. No single factor, other than the special blessings of God, contributed more to the growth and development of First Assembly, Memphis, than radio and television. In 1944 when I assumed the pastorate, none of the radio stations would sell the church time. The church was in a poor location with less than 100 members. It was during World War II; the newspapers limited churches to ads of one column inch per week.

I confess I was frustrated. In two of my former pastorates, I had daily radio programs and all the newspaper space we could afford. Now we were in a big city with a small group of people in a little building, poorly located, and had no way to tell the general public we were there. One day, in a moment of extreme discouragement,

I said to my wife, "If I live in this city until I die at a ripe old age, most people will never know I lived and worked here."

Finally in 1948, a small 250-watt radio station was built in Memphis, and we got in on the ground floor. After we had completed a year's contract, one of the 10,000-watt stations offered us a contract that led to a daily broadcast for several years and a weekly broadcast for more than thirty years! Over those years, we also had programs at various times on several other Memphis stations.

When television came to our city, First Assembly was the first church to purchase time and to have the first locally produced religious television program in the Midsouth. This program has continued for some thirty years. In addition, at various times we had different programs on three other television stations, some daily and some weekly.

More than sixteen years ago, a television panel show dealing with questions concerning the Bible and morals began and I was asked to serve on the first show. I still am on weekly. This program, called *What Is Your Faith?* has provided valuable publicity for the church and the pastor. According to a recent survey 55 percent of all Memphis TV sets are tuned in on Sunday morning. It should be no surprise that First Assembly is one of the best-known churches in the Midsouth.

Newspapers provide a means of getting the church before the public. E. S. Caldwell says, "One of the first places a minister needs to visit after accepting a new pastorate is the local newspaper." He goes on to list the kinds of stories the newspapers are more likely to print and suggests some things to do in publicizing an event.

Newspaper ads are expensive but very effective if properly designed and placed. The purpose of an ad is not to display talent, but to communicate. Caldwell adds, "It is doubtful there are many people who carefully read all church advertisements. People scan such ads, so the object is to catch and stop that scanning eye. That means there must be something unique about the wording of the ad. Perhaps it will be a thought provoking sermon title or a catchy phrase about the guest singing group. . . . The proposed copy for any ad should be examined with this question: If I were not from this church, is there something about the wording of this ad that might make me want to come?"[2] Ads should carefully display the exact date and time of the event.

There are other means of attracting people to the church ministry, including billboards and signs in strategic places.

It is also necessary to promote the church ministry within the church constituency. Perhaps the best way to do this is through the church bulletin, direct mail, a church newspaper, bulletin boards, and well-planned, succinct announcements.

The church newspaper is a very important means of providing information, instruction, and inspiration about the church, its ministry, coming events, special occasions, various activities, news about its people, and other valuable information. When publishing the church paper real care should be exercised in its layout, accuracy, grammar, overall coverage of the church interests, dates, and times.

Businesses take advantage of special days to promote and sell their products. Look at what they do for Mother's Day and Father's Day. They have so commercialized Christmas and Easter that these days have lost much of their significance for millions of people.

Jesus once said that the children of this world are wiser than the children of light. He meant that the children of this world take advantage of every opportunity to advance their cause while sometimes the children of light fail to do so. Let's take advantage of every situation and opportunity possible to reach a few more people with the gospel of Jesus Christ.

Such special days as Mother's Day, Father's Day, Easter, and Christmas are all naturals for church promotion. America has become church conscious on Easter and Christmas. Thousands of people who do not usually go to church go on these days. We need to take advantage of this tendency and get them in our church on these special occasions.

Mother's Day provides an opportunity to honor mothers, and often will result in many families coming to church to be with mother on her day. On Father's Day we used to encourage all fathers to invite their sons—and all sons to invite their fathers. We urged fathers to look around their neighborhood for a boy who was not attending church to bring him along as their adopted son. And we asked the boys to find a man in their neighborhood who did not attend church and to bring him as their adopted father. I recall a little boy coming up to me one Father's Day and saying, "Pastor, this is my adopted father for today. What do I do with him?"

There are many other days that can be successfully promoted:

installation, anniversaries, Memorial Day, a patriotic Sunday, home-coming, and so on. It is important that the church also promote special campaigns, evangelistic meetings, missionary conventions, and other events that are important to the church's growth and ministry.

Follow-Up

A church that ministers to the total family requires visitation. When our Heavenly Father sought Adam in the Garden the program of visitation was originated. When He became Immanuel it was established. He came "to seek and to save that which was lost." Visitation was practiced by the Early Church, who went from house to house breaking bread. It was the program of the New Testament church and resulted in the spread of Christianity.

Historians tell us that in one generation the church in Jerusalem grew from a handful of people to a membership of between twenty-five and one hundred thousand. How did they do it without radio, television, newspapers, magazines, and telephones? By word of mouth, personal witnessing, and personal visitation. Andrew brought Peter, John brought James, Philip brought Nathanael. This was the New Testament method.

Many years ago in Memphis, more than two hundred churches sponsored a spiritual renewal rally in the city auditorium. I was asked to serve as a member of the executive committee and as chairman of the church cooperation committee. My responsibilities included securing the cooperation of the churches and the attendance of their people. The newspapers became quite interested in this spiritual move and gave it front-page stories daily for about three weeks.

Mr. Edmond Meeman, editor of the *Memphis Press Scimitar*, was concerned about the attendance. He wrote to me that his long years of experience in sponsoring various types of meetings had taught him that no amount of publicity was as effective as a personal invitation. This observation from a newspaper editor points up once again that if we are going to reach the people for the church and for Christ, we must go after them personally.

After you get people started to church it is just as important to keep them going. We must give close attention to those who are absent. That's what Jesus taught with the parable of the ninety and nine sheep safe in the fold. The shepherd went out in search of the one lost sheep. All absentees must be followed up if we are to have a growing church. The absentee should be visited with the purpose of recovering him for the church. Do not be satisfied with just one visit; make as many as it takes to recover him. That is our business.

J. E. Connant tells of a terrible shipwreck off the coast of Italy. Instead of manning the lifeboats, the captain of the lifesaving crew stood on the shore and shouted instructions through a trumpet to the drowning sailors.

The report that went to the government said, "We rendered what assistance we could rough the speaking trumpet." But the next morning, twenty bodies washed ashore.

The pastor who tries to save his city and his world by simply serving as a "speaking trumpet" and fails to man the lifeboats of personal follow-up and visitation will be responsible for a great company of people who might have been saved.

Effective visitation is organized, systematic, and enthusiastic. The pastor of the church is responsible for the visitation program and must determine who makes visits, when a visit is made, on whom a visit is made, and record the results of such visits. Visitation must not be sporadic; it must be a planned, continuous program. Visitation must be personalized, demonstrating warmth and personal interest on the part of those who visit. We must guard against mechanical visitation. We must impress upon our workers that they are dealing with human souls, and failure at this point may cost the soul of someone that could have been reached.

Facilities

The location and facilities of a church are very important and contribute much to church growth. Great care should be taken in selecting a site for a church building. A feasibility study of the proposed site should be made. Local and area planning agencies can provide projections of future development in an area. A site most certainly should be on a well-known street with easy accessibility. If there must be a sacrifice of money, make it in the building rather than the location!

It is usually impossible to provide all the space and the facilities we desire, but in erecting a building, future expansion should be kept in mind in both the buying of the site (be sure it is larger than you presently need) and in the erection of the building. Build so you can expand without destroying your original building.

If we are to attract the general public, we must have facilities that are clean, well-kept, and as comfortable as we can make them. Present-day society is accustomed to comfort, and people are not likely to attend a church where they are physically uncomfortable.

Hard Work

An essential factor in church growth is hard work. There is no magic word or formula that will build a great, strong, Bible-believing, spiritual church. Hard work, long hours, self-denial, and sacrifice of leisure are necessary.

When Stewart Robinson, a well-known minister in the Assemblies of God, was a young preacher he asked me how to build a large church. I told him about a woman who once wrote to me and asked me to tell her in a few words how to build a large church. My answer was, "Dear Madam: In reply to your letter, work, work, work!—James E. Hamill."

We once had a young woman in our church apply for the position of bookkeeper in our church office. She was hired, but after some weeks she came in to my office and said, "Pastor, I am going to resign." I asked, "Why are you going to leave us so soon?" She replied, "This job isn't what I really expected it to be." Then I asked her, "What did you expect it to be?" Her reply was, "Well, it's a church and I thought that you met every day and prayed and sang songs, talked about the Lord and the blessings of God, but I discovered that you work, work, work!"

I endeavored to explain to her that we do work, and work hard, in order to win souls to Christ and establish them in the church and, thus, have a reason to sing and shout and praise the Lord.

Spirituality

In Acts 4 we have the spiritual factors in church growth. Peter and John had been arrested and imprisoned and the church had called a prayer meeting; it resulted in a tremendous spiritual experience for the people, as well as great growth for the church. The following spiritual elements for church growth are in Acts 4:

Prayer

Someone has said that a church advances on its knees. The person who does not pray does not grow in God. A church that does not pray does not grow. No prayer, no growth—for the individual or the church.

Prayer brings revival, revival results in spiritual renewal, spiritual renewal brings about witnessing and soul winning. This equals church growth.

Spirit-Filled

Many wonderful things followed the Jerusalem church's enduement with spiritual power: They spoke the Word of God with boldness, they were of one accord, great grace was upon them, with great power they gave witness, and they gave their material possessions to God through His church.

Acts 4 indicates that being filled with the Spirit is not a once and for all affair. Note one of the results of the prayer they offered when Peter and John returned from their appearance before the chief priests and elders: "They were all filled with the Holy Ghost"—that would include Peter and John!

Remember that Paul wrote the Ephesians, "Be filled with the Spirit" (Ephesians 5:18). According to Dr. Stanley Horton, "This (as the Greek indicates) is not a one-time experience, but a continued filling or (better) repeated fillings, as the Book of Acts suggests."[3]

Later in Acts the apostles recommend delegating a responsibility to others, with this guideline: "Brethren, look ye out among you seven men . . . full of the Holy Ghost" (6:3). They did, and we know the impact of at least one of these men: Stephen.

So we see this element in church growth. If the church is to have proper growth, it must have the power and the presence of the Holy Spirit. There is absolutely no substitute for the power of the Holy Spirit in church growth—which comes by being filled again and again.

Power To Witness

Acts 4:31 tells us that when they prayed and received the Holy

Spirit that they spoke the word "with boldness," and verse 33 says that "with great power gave the apostles witness of the resurrection."

They had prayed for this earlier: "Lord, grant unto thy servants, that with all boldness they may speak thy word . . . and that signs and wonders may be done by the name of thy holy child Jesus" (Acts 4:29,30).

The results of their bold and courageous preaching and witnessing, preaching God's Word and witnessing of Christ's resurrection, was, "Believers were the more added to the Lord, multitudes of both men and women" (Acts 5:14).

Real church growth cannot occur without courageous preaching and teaching of God's Word. Neither can there be much church growth without witnessing by the rank and file of the church.

The New Testament pattern for growth was preach the Word and every member a witness. This world will never be won to Christ from the pulpit alone. The task requires the effort of all of God's people, praying, witnessing, and working, giving of themselves, their time, their talent, and their money. The pastor is charged with the awesome responsibility of leading his people into a ministry of witnessing.

Great Grace

This growing New Testament church had "great grace upon them." That is, they became winsome Christians. They were fascinating, attractive Christians. They were an exciting group of people. They were enthusiastic about their resurrected Lord and about their church. They attracted the world rather than have the world attract them.

No one ever inquires of a griping, fault-finding, complaining, gossiping member how to know Jesus Christ, but a person is likely to inquire of the beautiful, fascinating, enthusiastic Christian how to be saved. The world is hungry for something real, genuine, warm, something worth getting excited about.

A woman came into my office one day and said, "My husband and I have been attending the services here for several months now, and we want to join this church." I told her we would be very happy to have them as members of the church. She continued, "I have gone to church all my life. My parents insisted that we go every service. As I grew up, I came to dislike church. My parents were critical of the preacher, the choir, the ushers, and everybody who participated in the meetings. I married a young man in the church who felt a great deal like I did, that our responsibility was to go to church even though we did not enjoy it. So, we have continued over the years. Some months ago we were invited to a service here at your church and came again and again. We have come to know the Lord Jesus Christ as Saviour and have discovered that it's a real joy and pleasure to attend church. We have not heard one complaint or one criticism, or anybody gossip about anybody else. This is the kind of church we want to join."

Willing Sharers

In studying the growth of the church, we discover the fact that a growing church is a giving church. The individual who grows in the grace and the knowledge of the Lord is a person who has learned stewardship, willing to share his material blessings with God through the church.

The church that has a missionary vision and gives to missions is more likely to grow than the church that does not.

When those first church members shared their possessions with the church, the infant church was able to report "the number of disciples were multiplied" (Acts 6:1); "believers were the more added to the Lord" (Acts 5:14); "and the Lord added to the church daily" (Acts 2:47).

United Believers

Acts 4:32 tells us that after being filled with the Holy Spirit the members of the growing, going, glowing church "were of one heart and one soul."

If a church is to grow it must be united. A divided house cannot stand, a divided army cannot march and fight, a divided team cannot win. For the church as well, unity is an absolute necessity.

If the pastor, under God, can lead his people into the fullness of the Holy Spirit with great grace upon them and the giving of their money and their witness, their church will be like the New Testament church that turned the world upside down, shook the Roman Empire, and established the church triumphant.

Substitutes for Spiritual Power

There are many substitutes for genuine growth in a church. In his attempt to lead his people in spiritual and numerical growth the pastor must avoid many quick fixes and apparent formulas.

In 1 Kings 14 is the story of Judah's apostasy under the reign of Rehoboam, Solomon's son. The Bible says Judah did evil in the sight of the Lord; the country provoked Him to jealousy. They built high places and images and groves, and "there were even male shrine prostitutes in the land" (1 Kings 14:24, NIV).

During this time of evil, idolatry, and immorality, Shishak, king of Egypt, attacked Jerusalem and took away the treasures of the house of the Lord; he took away all the shields of gold which Solomon had made. These were beautiful shields and they symbolized the prosperity with which God had blessed His people.

To hide his embarrassment, Rehoboam made shields of brass as substitutes for the shields of gold. He did not want the people or the other nations of the world to know that the shields of gold were gone. He tried to make brass look like gold.

It was and is the plan of God that the church of Jesus Christ be empowered by the Holy Spirit, that the Holy Spirit direct and empower the worship, the walk, and the work of the church, and that the church through the power of the Holy Spirit evangelize the world, build up the body of Christ, the church, and worship God.

But there are many substitutes for God's power in these days. Many things that are not necessarily bad in themselves become substitutes for spiritual growth and fall short of being the best of what God really wants for His church and His people.

Material Prosperity

At Pentecost, the church began with shields of gold. It had tremendous power with God and great influence over the people. In the face of all types of opposition from the established religious forces and a pagan government, a group of unknown but Spirit-filled and Spirit-empowered disciples of Jesus spread the gospel all over the known world.

Later the church joined hands with the world when the Roman emperor Constantine embraced Christianity. The church then relaxed its pursuit of holiness and became worldly, sinful, and weak.

The church learned that it is a colossal error to believe that with material prosperity, with silver and gold, it could buy the conquest of a sinful world. If the church had all the money in the world, controlled all the wealth on earth, it could not compel men to accept and live for Jesus Christ.

Only the power of the Holy Spirit can change the hearts of men and can work out God's will, plan, program, in the life of the individual and in the corporate life of the church.

The Laodicean church felt that it had reached the apex when it became financially independent. They were rich, increased in goods, and thought they had need of nothing. But Jesus' analysis of the church was entirely different. He said, "Thou art wretched, and miserable, and poor, and blind, and naked" (Revelation 3:17). They had tried to substitute material wealth for spiritual power. This cannot be done.

Church Activities

I am a firm believer in an aggressive church. I believe in activity on the part of Christians. I do not subscribe to a passive religion. I believe that Christianity is vigorous, progressive, militant, alive, active; but the fact remains that much church activity today is simply brass trying to shine like gold.

Sardis was such a church. It had a name that said it lived. But Jesus told John in Revelation that the church at Sardis was dead. The Lord did not mean that all activities of the church had ceased. It had a reputation for activity. In fact, it had been so busy that it hadn't realized that it was dead. The church, no doubt, still had all of its meetings, its committees, its auxiliaries, its youth activities, its socials, its suppers.

This is not to say that a church shouldn't have these things. In many cases, they are a valuable part of a good church program. But these things are minors, not majors. Any time a church majors in these minors, and gives more time to these secondary matters than to prayer meetings, revival services, outreach ministries, personal evangelism, and church visitation, it is missing the mark.

It is possible to become so absorbed in the activities of the program that we allow them to become substitutes for the power of the Holy Spirit. There must be activity if we are to fulfill our Lord's commission to carry the gospel to the ends of the earth. But we must have the Holy Spirit directing and empowering us.

Intellectualism

We live in a day of an unprecedented quest for education. This is the most sophisticated, best educated, most knowledgeable generation in the history of the world. This is good if that knowledge, that education, is Christ-centered, or if the recipient of such knowledge is grounded in the eternal truth of God.

The apostle Paul warned us, "Beware lest any man spoil you through philosophy and vain deceit, after the tradition of men, after the rudiments of the world, and not after Christ" (Colossians 2:8).

The great apostle also talked about men being "vain in their imaginations and their foolish heart [being] darkened. Professing themselves to be wise, they became fools" (Romans 1:21,22). A false philosophy is known by its purely human origin. All human knowledge is imperfect: "If any man think that he knoweth anything, he knoweth nothing yet as he ought to know" (1 Corinthians 8:2).

The traditions of men are the accumulation of mere human theories transmitted from age to age until they have assumed the pretentions of a philosophy imposing a number of uninspired, unauthorized observations and liturgies. So a philosophy that builds solely on man is baseless and full of danger.

A false philosophy is known by its Christlessness, "not after Christ," as Paul put it. Christ is neither the author nor the substance of its teaching. Such philosophy relies on human intelligence and human traditions, substituting man's reasoning for the clear-cut statements made in God's Word.

This, however, is not an argument for ignorance. I have never seen but one man who had all the education that he thought he needed. This man said that he prayed that God would make him more ignorant, and I replied, "Brother, that's one prayer God cannot answer. You are just as ignorant as you can be."

But as valuable as education is in our world today, and I would not minimize it for a moment, unless it is Christ-centered and Holy Ghost anointed, it is only brass substituting for gold. It will not accomplish the eternal task that is ours, as followers of Jesus Christ, in building the church of our Lord.

Sensationalism

To be sensational is not necessarily wrong. Jesus was sensational—not because He tried to be but by nature of what He was: the Son of God who had become the Son of Man, God wrapped in human flesh walking among men.

Sensationalism becomes wrong, very wrong, when we permit it to be a substitute for the power of God.

Sensationalism, as it relates to the work of God, is putting the emphasis in the wrong place and emphasizing the physical by-product of the presence and power and glory of God.

For example, when the Holy Spirit came upon the disciples on the Day of Pentecost and the one hundred and twenty received the infilling of the Holy Spirit, we are told that "suddenly there came a sound from heaven as of a rushing mighty wind, and it filled all the house where they were sitting. And there appeared unto them cloven tongues as of fire, and it sat upon each of them" (Acts 2:2,3).

The fire and the wind are not the important part of this story; the vital statement is, "They were all filled with the Holy Ghost" (Acts 2:4).

If this outpouring of the Holy Spirit at Pentecost were to be reported today, many people would have as the headline: "There was a mighty rushing wind and tongues of fire!" Little attention would probably be given to the one hundred twenty whose lives were filled with the power of God.

Do you realize that after that day the apostles never did refer to the mighy rushing wind and the tongues of fire? They did refer to people receiving the Holy Spirit; they did refer to people speaking in tongues—that was the important part of the story—that one hundred twenty people were filled with the dynamic power of the Holy Spirit.

In Acts 4, the Scriptures tell us that "when they prayed, the place was shaken where they were assembled together and they were all filled with the Holy Ghost" (v. 31).

Now, the sensational part of that story is that the house literally shook, but the important part of the story is that they were all filled with the Holy Ghost; they spoke the Word of God with boldness;

they had all things in common; and great grace was upon them. The important part of the story was what happened inside the disciples, not what happened outside.

It is so unfortunate that many sincere Christians endeavor to live on sensationalism. They are influenced and overwhelmed by sensationalists, those who claim way-out manifestations.

The wilder the story the more godly the person, according to the thinking of these unfortunate victims of sensationalism. These sensational stories have to get bigger and bigger and wilder and wilder to get the people's attention. Those who feed upon this kind of thing lose their appetite for the real Word of God, and actually forget what the real manifestation of the Holy Spirit is like.

As a young boy in rural Mississippi, one of my chores on our farm was to feed the pigs. I can recall so clearly pouring a basket of corn into the pig trough and seeing a little runt pig rush up to the trough and grab a nubbin and start running around the pen squealing as though he had the corner on the corn crop of the world. Would you believe that those pigs would leave all that fine corn in the trough and take out chasing that runt of a pig with only a nubbin? I thought, *Surely hogs are the dumbest of all animals.*

Now I'm not sure, for I've seen people chase after spiritual runts screaming about a "nubbin" they possess.

No amount of sensationalism is a substitute for the real power of the Holy Spirit. We must not substitute anything for the reality of the presence and power of God. We must have God's power to enjoy genuine church growth.

Emotionalism

I would not pay taxes on a religious experience that did not affect my emotions. I believe that Christianity is an emotional religion. The soul is the seat of our emotions and our affections. Our faith comes to grips with both the mind and the heart.

Nevertheless, however desirable it may be to have an emotional expression of our love for God and to be emotionally moved in our worship, this is not a substitute for the power of the Holy Spirit working in our lives and in our church. To have an emotional experience is not the culmination of the fullness of the Holy Spirit; it is a by-product.

Demonstrations for some have become a substitute for the real power of the Holy Spirit. Demonstrations that are in order are good, but they must not become a substitute for the real moving of the Holy Spirit in our lives and in our church services. Orchestration and manipulation of so-called worship by the pastor, or anyone else, is a poor substitute for the power of God. It is brass trying to shine like gold.

The Good for the Best

Now brass is not bad. Brass probably made some very beautiful shields. But brass is only good; gold is best. Rehoboam was substituting the good for the best. If Satan cannot get us to take the worst, then many times he will offer us a substitute for the best. The substitute might not be bad, it might even be good, but it is not the best. God wants us to have the best.

We are saying that prosperity is good, don't fight it. Church activity is necessary, don't condemn it. To develop the mind is great, don't downgrade it. Emotionalism is important, don't rule it out. All these things are good, but they must not become substitutes for the best. They must not become brass trying to shine like gold.

The pastor plays a tremendous part in the spiritual and numerical growth of the church as he provides leadership in recruiting, training, and directing personnel; as he organizes and promotes the church, follows up the prospects and members; as he leads in providing facilities; as he sets an example in hard work and inspires others to do likewise.

But his most effective leadership in church growth is in the spiritual area where he leads the people to pray; encourages the church to be filled with the Spirit and to boldly witness for Christ; where he encourages the people to manifest the fruit of the Spirit, to give their money to God through the church, and to be of one mind and one accord; and where he preaches God's Word boldly and with faith.

NOTES

[1]Thomas F. Zimmerman, ed., *And He Gave Pastors* (Springfield, MO: Gospel Publishing House, 1979), p. 401.

[2]Ibid., p. 402, 414.

[3]Stanley M. Horton, *What the Bible Says About the Holy Spirit* (Springfield, MO: Gospel Publishing House, 1976), p. 244.